Praise for *Victory Under Pressure*

"Life is full of opportunities, trials and pressures. Oftentimes, people succumb to the pressures of life, feeling as if there are no answers. Most people have big ideas, big dreams or even big visions; however, when the pressures of life come, these ideas, dreams and visions often dissipate into thin air. In *Victory Under Pressure*, my wife explores the life of Joseph and offers divine direction to every reader on how to achieve the goals set before him or her. After reading this book, my heart was overjoyed, knowing that even in the midst of pressure, God has answers for every situation, and that victory belongs to me. I encourage you to read this book and set your compass for a destination called *victory!*"

-Dr. Hardie Davis Jr., Senior Pastor, Abundant Life Worship Center
Augusta, Georgia

"Today's Christians live in a whirlwind of challenges and adversities, and they desire victory in their lives. Evett Davis has a compassionate heart for the needs of people from all walks of life. *Victory Under Pressure* is a timely book; a must-read for every Believer."

-Bishop Kenneth & Gloria Fuller

"In some ways, we all have had our share of disappointments, challenges and adversities. *Victory Under Pressure* is an outstanding book, because it gives you exactly what you need to defeat and overcome hopelessness. Evett Davis has done an excellent job in sharing her personal experiences of defeat and, most importantly, victory. Many Christians give up on living a life of victory, because they can't get past their failures. This book will take you on a journey of victories so that although you may be living under life's pressures, victory can become your lifestyle!"

-Ministers Reginald & Wantá Ezell

"For those whose destination is victory, this book gives clear direction on how to get there and stay there. Truly an inspiration and challenge. It is an excellent tool for evaluating our relationship with God, and whether or not we are truly living victoriously. Once you start reading this book, you don't want to stop. Once you finish, you want to start traveling this road to victory!"

-Shirley A. Ledbetter, Administrator,
Beacon Institute of Ministry

"A cat always lands on its feet. Why? It first gets its head straight with its surroundings and its feet quickly follow. In much the same way, Evett Davis in her book, *Victory Under Pressure,* helps us to get our thinking straight so that victory can follow. This book is for those who want more out of life. Evett is passionate about helping others to endure life's pressure and to be elevated to the position of victors!

-David L. Baldwin, D.Min., Ever Forward Ministries
Merriam, Kansas

"Victory Under Pressure is a must read for the body of Christ and the unsaved. Evett Davis has used the story of Joseph, along with her personal testimony, to highlight what it means to live a victorious life. As the pressures of life continue to build every day, having the ability to utilize the tools of the Holy Spirit, vision, faithfulness, favor and forgiveness will prepare God's people to achieve victory under pressure. Kudos for this blessed book that is sensitive to the end times."

-Dr. Philip M. Dunston, Faculty and Program Director,
Clark Atlanta University,
Department of Religion and Philosophy

"Superb job! Evett Davis puts her message in practical, everyday terms for every born-again Believer. This is an inspiring book to propel anyone toward their God-ordained destiny."

-Stacy Arrington, Davidson Fine Arts Magnet School,
Augusta, Georgia

"As you read this book in its entirety, you will see how it can transform your mindset. Evett Davis talks about different challenges an individual may face in life, family, career and so on. She examines the life of the biblical figure Joseph who is a perfect example. No matter what obstacles, hindrances or challenges he faced, God always caused him to triumph. Joseph was faced with setbacks, but by expressing God's character throughout his life, he was able to prevail. He walked in favor, forgiveness, love, patience and the wisdom of God. This book will strengthen your faith, help you see your dreams become a reality, and inspire you to possess victory on every side."

-**Pastors Sidney & Barbara Payton,**
Glory Church International, Columbia,
South Carolina

VICTORY

UNDER PRESSURE

Learning How to Win Big in Life!

VICTORY

UNDER PRESSURE

Learning How to Win Big in Life!

EVETT DAVIS

Victory Under Pressure: Learning How to Win Big in Life!
©2005 by Evett Davis
P.O. Box 6149
Augusta, Georgia 30916

Printed in the United States of America

ISBN 978-0-9773832-0-7

Publishing and interior design by GUMM Publishing Group
www.gummpublishing.com

Cover design by Higher Impact Designs, Inc., Tulsa, Oklahoma
www.higherimpactdesigns.com

Contents

Dedication

To my husband, Hardie and our son, "Prince" Benjamin.
I am grateful for the unconditional, God-kind of love that you
share with me daily. Your love, prayers and support allow me to
do what the Lord directs me to do with ease. I am thankful to
Him for the opportunity to share and experience life in the
overflow with you two awesome men of God. I love you!

Foreword

"...And this is the victory that overcometh the world, even our faith"
(1 John 5:4)

According to the Bible, a lot of crazy things will happen in life; but if you know what the Bible says, you can make those difficult situations work out for your good. This book on the life of Joseph by Evett Davis shows us how God can make a bad situation work out for our good so that we don't have to live like victims of the world we live in.

Like many of us, Joseph experienced many obstacles and challenges. He went from living in the comfort of his own home with his family, to being thrown into a pit, sold into slavery, lied about and thrown into prison. The end result, however, is that he obtained the victory. He overcame his adversities and won.

We encounter obstacles and are faced with challenges almost every day. Sometimes it can be very overwhelming and difficult to face them, especially when you don't know what to do. Nonetheless, there are answers to life's challenges. These answers are found in the Word of God and can be seen in the experiences of others. Like Joseph, we can overcome adversity by exercising our faith in God.

By looking at the life of Joseph we can see all of the obstacles and challenges he had to face, and learn from how he overcame them by holding on to the covenant promises he had from God. The Lord gave him a vision, which was the driving force necessary for Joseph to overcome his adversities. Joseph's life is an example of how to maintain the victory through faith in God.

Evett really unfolds the life of Joseph in this book to let us all know that, like Joseph, we can overcome through our faith in God. We are given insight and answers as we examine real life examples.

Therefore, whatever situations you maybe facing right now, you need answers on how to overcome and how to become a world overcomer. Jesus says in John 16:33 *"...In the world ye shall have tribulation: but be of good cheer; I have overcome the world."* Jesus, like Joseph, faced a lot of obstacles and challenges. He was betrayed by a disciple for thirty pieces of silver, lied about and thrown in the pit of hell. But, he did not allow those adversities to stop Him from fulfilling God's will for His life. Like Joseph, Jesus went from the pit to the palace, which is the very throne room of God.

Victory Under Pressure will give you the answers you need to help you to overcome and move from a place of defeat to a place of victory in every area of life. You'll learn how to set priorities in life in order to stay focused on the will of God. You will be reminded of the covenant that you have with God—a covenant of blessings and favor. Knowing that God is the source for all of your needs, I believe your relationship with God will become stronger. I know that by the end of this book you will step into the winner's circle with the victory to overcome every challenge!

—Tony and Cynthia Brazelton

Acknowledgements

There are many people who have impacted my life in very meaningful ways. Their influence, love and encouragement mean the world to me.

I thank my Creator and Sustainer for choosing me for such a time as this. Dr. Creflo A. Dollar and Taffi L. Dollar, the greatest spiritual parents in the world, have imparted, impacted and inspired me through their teaching of the Word of God.

A special thanks to my husband, Hardie, and our son, Benjamin, for their love that ignited the energy that I needed to complete this project.

I would like to thank Patricia Copeland, my mother, for enduring the pressures of life. Through her, I learned to keep pushing and pressing until I achieve the results I desire. I love her!

Leroy Copeland, you came into our lives, married mom, and took us to another level. You are an awesome man that I will forever admire.

Thanks to my other father and mother, Hardie Sr. and Delois Davis. I appreciate your love and unconditional support for all that we do.

I thank my loving family and friends for the experiences in life that we share. Thanks goes to my Aunt Ludell for being the pillar of faith, prayer and love for our entire family.

I would like to thank Pastors Tony and Cynthia Brazelton for continuing to share the heart, wisdom and love of God with my husband and me. Their success as pastors is an inspiration, and I am grateful to God for the anointing that is on their lives.

Thanks Ministers Reginald and Wantá Ezell, Bishop Kenneth and Mother Gloria Fuller, and Pastors Sidney and Barbara Payton for the wisdom that you continue to unconditionally impart into our lives and our ministry.

Thanks goes to a special person who I'll refer to as my Covenant Friend. She is an awesome woman of God who diligently ministers to me and encourages me with the Word of God when I am faced with the internal and external pressures of life.

I would like to thank Sheila Jones of Prevailing Word Transcription Ministry who made this project easier by transcribing my teachings.

Words of gratitude to my editor, Oscar Camejo Jr. of GUMM Publishing Group, for his anointed insight and publishing assistance. My brother, you are definitely graced to do what you do. I thank God for bringing us together for this project.

Thanks to Ron King of Higher Impact Designs for your persistence and creativity. You have done an awesome job with the cover design of this project.

I would like to thank my other set of "fresh eyes" for reviewing this project: Stacy Arrington, Sherry Bennett and BJ Blackwood. May the favor of God be upon you for rendering your time in reviewing this project.

Lastly, I would like to thank the members of Abundant Life Worship Center for all of their support. They are absolutely the best!

Introduction

I have been pressured to quit my entire life. Talk about having the odds stacked against you. People and adverse circumstances have tried their best to destroy my self-esteem and ultimately my destiny. However, despite life's pressures I did not give up or cave in. Reflecting over my life, I can now smile because I am living the life of a winner. I am victorious and my future gets brighter every day!

It took some time and hard work to get where I am today emotionally, spiritually and mentally. I have had many not-so-bright days. Growing up in a single parent home was not easy. My mother, Patricia Copeland, gave birth to four girls, of which I am the third born. She had her share of life's pressures, especially having to work three jobs while my grandmother took care of us. I recall seeing the daily physical, mental and emotional exhaustion on my mother's face as a result of her working all day to provide the basic necessities for our family. There were days when she would be away from home the entire day every day, and it was those days that I missed her the most.

Children need constant nurturing from both of their parents. In my case, my father was not around to do his part, and my mother did the best she could at the time. Raising four girls was not a piece of cake, but she found a way and I am grateful for her sacrifice. Through her example, I learned how to never allow defeat to have the last word. Her determination and resolve have been the torches that have helped to guide me through life's darkness. When the future looked bleak, these torches illuminated my path toward victory.

This book was born out of my journey through the darkness of life and what I learned about living victoriously in the midst of adversity. No one wants to experience hardships in life. No one wants to struggle while pursuing his or her dreams. We all desire to run this race without becoming fatigued by the pressures of relationships, finances, careers and so on. Some people settle for whatever life throws their way. Their mentality is, *I'll accept whatever cards life deals to me.* That is how defeated people think. Hopefully this is not your attitude toward life. Winners don't settle for last place and they don't compromise their chances for victory; instead, they do whatever it takes to take home the winning prize!

Your response toward adversity will determine your success or failure. I don't believe for one moment that you consciously desire to fail. Yes, you may feel as if you're in last place in this race of life. You may feel like quitting; however, don't allow *feelings* to govern your life. Negative feelings will cause you to cave in when disappointment shows up.

Life may be full of disappointments, so what! Develop confidence in who you are and discover what you are destined to accomplish. Your destiny is waiting for you to fulfill it.

You may be defeat-minded now, but after you read this book, you will be *victory-minded.* Victory-minded people don't run from or ignore adversity; instead, they face them. Like a track runner preparing for the biggest race of your life, you must develop a vision of success. Why? Because victory starts with a vision. The pressure is on. Other runners are taunting you. Thoughts of past losses may be filling your mind. You may be considered the "underdog" in this race. Quit or run the race...what will you do?

While reading this book, you will be challenged to think like an athlete. No one is born an award-winning athlete; instead, they are trained and developed to win. I included an entire chapter on establishing a connection with your ultimate personal trainer, God, and how a healthy relationship with Him is essential to your success in life. How you relate to Him makes all the difference. People who are faithful to God reap the rewards of faithfulness: prosperity, promotion and protection. Don't you want this to be the testimony of your life? Sure you do. As your personal trainer, God wants you to win big; but, winning has a price tag. It takes discipline and faithfulness to win the prize. There are no shortcuts to victory.

You are in an endurance race that will either make you or break you. You can win it as you continue pressing on and hurdling all of the obstacles that are designed to slow you down. Have you ever heard the statement, "It's not how you start, it's how you finish"? This is true when it comes to running life's race and winning.

The Apostle Paul once wrote, *"Do you not know that in a race all the runners compete, but [only] one receives the prize? So run [your race] that you may lay hold [of the prize] and make it yours"* (1 Corinthians 9:24, *The Amplified Bible*). In line with Paul, my message to you is to run your race with confidence, knowing that there is a great prize waiting for you at the finish line. With God on your side, you are favored to win. That is the heartbeat of *Victory Under Pressure*.

The Spirit of Victory

1

1

The Spirit of Victory

"For whatsoever is born of God overcometh the world: and this is the victory that overcometh the world, even our faith"(1 John 5:4).

Have you ever watched the Olympic games? There is always plenty of excitement as hundreds of athletes from around the world compete in dozens of sports, each representing their country, each wanting to win the gold medal. Those watching from the sidelines are eager to see their fellow country men win, and often embrace strangers in exhilarated moments of victory.

The history of the Olympic games, which is said to date as far back as 776 B.C., is very interesting. The victor in those days would receive an award immediately after the competition and a herald, or announcer, would declare his win publicly. The herald would then place a palm branch in the victor's hand, while spectators threw flowers to him. Red ribbons would be tied to his head and hands. Finally, on the last day of the Games, the herald would place a sacred olive tree wreath on the winner's head. Today's crowning ceremonies are no less glorious. Olympic winners receive medals of gold, silver or bronze, and are celebrated worldwide.

Think about the Olympics for a moment in comparison to

your journey through life. In the track and field events, there are various foot races including sprints, middle distance and long distance races. These races are designed to test speed and endurance. Likewise, life involves various sprints, middle distance races and long distances races, so to speak.

A *sprint* is simply a short distance race ran at full speed. In life, sprints represent the everyday decisions you make concerning your job or business, friends, relatives, personal finances, self-development and so forth. Because you probably live a very busy life, oftentimes you may not be able to give as much attention to these important areas as you would like. But imagine having quick wins in these areas all of the time. After all, small victories lead to great victories. For example, deciding to mend a broken relationship with a coworker or friend today is a small, yet significant victory. If you have poor spending habits, saving $30 to $50 this weekend rather than spending it on eating out or on entertainment, is a victory.

In each of these scenarios, you can make the wrong decision and achieve the same negative results that you may be accustomed to. As you "sprint" every day, you will be pressured to make decisions based on your emotions rather than on sound judgment. However, there is something awesome about making God-inspired decisions and achieving small victories. A sense of accomplishment will fill your heart and motivate you to continue pressing on toward the big victories.

Running the *middle distance race*s of life involves decision-making regarding short-term goals. These kinds of decisions should never be impulsive. For example, you shouldn't rush into buying a new car, resigning from a job, relocating to a new state, starting a business, or deciding whether or not to put your children in public or private school. You may be pressured on all sides to make these kinds of decisions. Your loved ones may be pressuring you to move forward with a decision that you are not ready to make. They may mean the best; however, never rush or else you will get into trouble if you do. Just as it takes time and effort to complete an 800 or 1,500-meter race, it takes effort and time to successfully achieve your short-term goals.

What about life's *long-distance races*? Take, for example, getting married, raising children, purchasing a home, writing a book, or pursuing your lifelong dreams. These medium to long-term goals are all achievable for the most part. Circumstances may tell you otherwise; however, what *you* and God perceive about your future makes all the difference.

Your life may seem like a marathon, with the finish line nowhere in sight. Perhaps the pressure to quit is stronger today than it has ever been. Negative thoughts, like cramps in the legs of a tired runner, may be slowing you down.

> "...THERE IS SOMETHING AWESOME ABOUT MAKING GOD-INSPIRED DECISIONS AND ACHIEVING SMALL VICTORIES."

Blood, sweat and tears are evidence of your hard work. What are you prepared to do to win this long distance race of life?

With preparation, discipline and endurance, you will bring home the gold medal in each major "event" (or aspect) of your life—family, relationships, finances, career, spirituality, etc. Despite the challenges you may have encountered, you can succeed in each of these areas, no questions asked. You will be rewarded for accomplishing your divine purpose.

What were you born to accomplish? What is your life's passion? No one else in the entire world has *your* specific assignment. Your destiny, regardless of what it is, is linked to God's ultimate plan for your life. The question is, are you ready to do whatever it takes to run this race and follow His plan?

No Pain, No Gain

Before embarking on the search for your destiny, it is important to understand a very simple concept that sometimes eludes many Christians. Challenges *do* come. Challenges are simply pressures of life that can come in different ways, mainly in the form of *internal* and *external* pressures.

The American Heritage® Dictionary of the English Language, Fourth Edition defines *pressure* as "an oppressive condition of physical, mental, social or economic distress." *Merriam-Webster's Medical Dictionary* defines it as "the burden of mental or physical distress especially from grief, illness, or adversity."

To understand *internal* and *external* pressures, picture a small to medium-sized circle. That circle simply represents your life. There are people who live inside of your circle and some who live outside. Your inner circle is comprised of friends and loved ones—those who have a greater potential to influence your life than those on the outside. Outer circle people are those who are not close to you. You interact with them occasionally at work, in the grocery store, at school and other places.

It is said that those who are closest to us can hurt us the most. I know this firsthand. Much of the hurt that I experienced growing up came from my inner circle of influence. Being ridiculed by others was common for me. The emotional strain that I experienced at a young age was tremendous. Through all of the hurt and pain, I emerged victorious.

Many Christians believe that once they become "born again" or "saved," they will no longer experience challenges. This couldn't be farther from the truth. In fact, thinking this way will cause Believers to neglect preparing themselves for the race of their lives.

Think about Jesus for a moment and the time of preparation He went through that helped Him to win the victory in His life. He knew what it meant to triumph in the midst of adversity. Jesus gave His disciples a clue concerning enduring adversity. He told them that although challenges would come, they should be of good cheer (John 16:33). They could live as overcomers by following His example.

This is an interesting concept, especially when looking at the life of the average Christian. I believe that many born-again Believers allow the pressures of life to defeat them because they don't understand this concept. Allow me to explain.

Since we live in the world, we are automatically faced with temptations like other human beings. However, what separates Christians from those who are not born again is the fact that Jesus has given us His Spirit to help us overcome the problems we face. Simply put, our victory is in Him.

In Psalm 34:19, God said it this way: *"Many are the afflictions of the righteous: but the Lord delivereth him out of them all."* That is what Jesus was talking about. It's as if He told the disciples, "I know that you will face many challenges, but don't worry. If you come to Me, I will show you how to overcome them. I have figured out a way to solve all of those challenges." So being of good cheer simply means to have hope because you know that the tribulation or challenge you are facing will be of short duration. When you look at challenges from this perspective, you can become victory minded.

Victory-minded people don't accept defeat, regardless of the adversity. Instead, they only think about winning. That is what you must do—think about winning in every area of life. When you are pressured by loved ones and friends to give up on your dreams, think victory. When your company undergoes a period of downsizing, think victory. Use every situation as an opportunity to think victory. Remember, you're in a "footrace" that is testing your endurance. In fact, think of this race as a *steeplechase*: a race run by people over a course that features obstacles and barriers. You have what it takes to endure the pressure to quit. You have the inner fortitude to hurdle the obstacles and burst through the barriers of life. You're a winner!

Preparing for the Race

A practical way to understand the mechanics of overcoming pressure is to look at the stages a person goes through before becoming an accomplished, award-winning runner. Each stage contains positive and negative elements that can be compared to the life of a Christian. At each stage, there are warning signs that if ignored by the runner, will cause him or her to quit eventually. These stages are *The Beginner, The Jogger, The Competitor, The Athlete* and *The Runner* stages.

The Beginner Stage

At this stage, the excitement of something new causes a person to be full of energy and enthusiasm. The Beginner often has no vision of the type of course he wants to run. He is simply content with getting off of the couch and getting into shape.

A Beginner (or "Baby Christian") is one who may have been a churchgoer for a long time, but really has no understanding of the spiritual power that was made available to him. A phrase like "authority in Christ" may mean nothing to him. He will get easily frustrated and argue to get his way. He is content with just attending church when the weather is favorable and will give an offering once in a while. He has no real sense of purpose in his life, and easily becomes distracted from spending time with God.

This type of Christian may get excited at the prospect of a "church convention," but will only attend the sessions whose times are convenient. When attempting to pursue things that he knows are good for him (whether it is reading the Bible or eating healthy), he will quit if these things cause him too much discomfort. This Christian needs others to direct him and is uncomfortable with praying for others.

The Jogger Stage

The Jogger is more comfortable with running. He is slowly starting to enjoy the benefits of getting into shape and spends less time with friends who may not understand this new lifestyle of running. Like the Beginner, he still does not have a set plan for running, but what distinguishes him is that he will feel guilty for skipping a run.

The Jogger can be compared to the Christian who makes minimal strides toward achieving his spiritual goals. Regular church attendance is slowly becoming a lifestyle. He begins to see moderate changes in his attitude toward God and others. Just as jogging helps to improve the cardiovascular condition of the heart, spiritual exercise, such as prayer, reading the Bible and regular church attendance, help to improve a Christian's love walk.

The Competitor Stage

Once a Jogger begins to establish a routine and has learned to disregard tiredness and discomfort to continue running, he becomes The Competitor. He must, however, be sure of his motives. Why? Because oftentimes he may overexert himself by running faster, longer races, always striving to outdo others. At this point, he loses his passion and no longer enjoys running. because all of the fun has been taken away; competing simply becomes nothing more than a way to obtain trophies.

How many born-again Believers do you know who seem to always compete against other Believers for attention and recognition? They compete for an audience with their pastors. They compete for the "I drive the best car and live in the best house" award. Sadly, they are engaging in competitive jealousy brought on by internal and external pressures, and their lives are in shambles as a result.

The Athlete Stage

Not all runners go through the competitive stage. Many bypass this stage to become athletes. The athlete's motivation is to fulfill his potential. He is aware of his limits as well as capabilities, and does what is necessary to achieve successful results. This means he will spend time planning and becoming familiar with the racecourse.

Likewise, when you are sure of your potential to win big in life, you do not have to compete for attention or recognition. Your race in life is to please God and Him only. As a spiritual athlete, you strive for perfection in order to live the life that He destined for you to live.

The Runner Stage

A perfect balance of the four stages produces an accomplished runner. Running is now a part of the runner's everyday activities, like breathing, sleeping and eating. He is comfortable with where he is and may spend time helping others achieve their goals in running. He no longer allows the stresses of the race to distract him; instead, he uses running as an opportunity to relieve stress and to continue building endurance.

The Runner does not need anyone to motivate him to run; he has long settled the importance of running in his life and has already experienced its benefits. He is like the runner Paul describes in Hebrews 12:1 who has learned to lay aside every weight and to run with patience the race that is set before him, and he holds fast to his convictions. To *hold fast* in the Greek comes from the word *katecho*. This word is a compound of two words: *kata* meaning "to come down with force," and *echo* meaning "to have or possess."

In essence, the accomplished runner represents the Christian who knows and understands the power he has available to him, and uses it in every opportunity. Even when he hears news that may seem threatening, his first response is to hold fast to the promises God has made, and patiently expect a positive outcome.

Responding to Pressure

We all desire to make the right decisions in life so that we can experience positive outcomes. Unfortunately, not all of us are prepared to face the problems that come to distract us. Problems have nothing to do with how spiritual, how committed or how dedicated a person is. They are simply just a part of life. Your response in times of trouble makes all the difference.

How do you view problems? You can either look at them as hindrances or springboards to propel you toward accomplishing your goals. **I encourage you to see problems as victories in the making.** That is how victory-minded people think.

Sometimes people look at ministers or people who have accomplished great things like Ghandi or Mother Theresa, and wonder how they found the strength to overcome their challenges. The answer is simple.

When people are faced with adversity, they have the choice to respond one of three ways: they can **run**, **ignore** or **face** their challenges. These responses are defense mechanisms that people most often learn during their childhood. Some are comfortable with ignoring problems, hoping they will eventually go away. Some run from adversity by resigning from a job impulsively, moving to another state to "start over," or prematurely ending a marriage. Others choose to face their challenges head-on and resolve them no matter how difficult they are.

This is where being a Christian causes a person to have an advantage over their problems, especially if this is a Believer who is aware of his power and authority. Let's discuss a typical scenario to see how the three different responses (run, ignore or face) can cause a person to experience victory or defeat.

> **"BEGIN TO SEE PROBLEMS AS VICTORIES IN THE MAKING."**

Many Christians and non-Christians alike experience challenges with debt, for example. In a society where purchasing things by using credit seems to be the method of choice, people often find themselves in a sea of debt that seems to overwhelm them and cause them to drown financially. Those who choose to run from financial problems will avoid answering their telephone, especially when a creditor's name appears on the caller ID. Does this scenario sound familiar? Some people conveniently "forget" to give their creditors a forwarding address when they move. I am sure that we all know friends or relatives who have done this, or maybe we have done this ourselves.

The outcome for this type of response to challenges is always negative. Not only do credit agencies have the means to locate them, but by the time they do so, interest rates have increased on their accounts to such an extent that it has doubled or even tripled the principal balance. If this describes you, it's time to "face the music."

Next, we have those people who ignore problems. These are people who continue to live life as if they are not in trouble. They ignore the stresses in their marriage. They ignore the fact their children are failing in school. Basically, they figure that ignoring their issues long enough would somehow make them go away. Unfortunately, it doesn't work that way. Ignore a small problem today, and it will hibernate for a while until it grows into a monstrous dilemma in the future.

Last, we have those individuals who decide to face the mountain of their problems, no matter how huge the mountain is. In the past, they may have been a part of the first or second group mentioned above, but have finally decided to take responsibility for their decisions. They take the time to face the truth about their dilemmas. The truth of the matter is that you need to know where you are so that you can know where you're going.

Truth be told, all three groups of people know that ignoring or running from a problem always causes greater issues in the long run. So why choose those responses anyway? I believe that many people simply lack hope. The Word of God says, *"Hope deferred makes the heart sick..."* (Proverbs 13:12, *AMP*). Heartsickness is no easy feeling, especially if you feel too weak to stand your ground when the pressures of life are weighing heavily on you.

A Christian who is unsure of God's love for him or her, and who spends little time reading His promises, will no doubt find it difficult to face a problem head on and bear up under pressure. He, too, will run, ignore and be defeated in every area of life, not knowing that the answer is available to everyone who seeks it.

How does a person go from ignoring problems or running from them, to facing them with courage? The answer is found in changing your mindset. Once a person realizes and accepts the fact that Jesus died for them to overcome their situation, hope begins to replace fear and dread. This person becomes more open to receiving instructions from God, and begins to make sound decisions.

Slowly but surely, this person goes from fearing the challenge and running from it, to facing it with boldness, knowing that God is there to assist and comfort him. Hebrews 10:23, in *The Amplified Bible*, says, "*So let us seize and hold fast and retain without wavering the hope we cherish and confess and our acknowledgement of it, for He Who promised is reliable (sure) and faithful to His word.*"

Hope for the Future

My desire for you is that you find hope in your future. Whether you are a Christian or not, God wants to help you live a good life as you pursue the fulfillment of your destiny. In Ephesians 2:4-5, Paul says this about God: "*But God, who is rich in mercy, for his great love wherewith he loved us, even when we were dead in sins, hath quickened us together with Christ....*" This means that although a person has yet to give his life over to God, God's desire doesn't change. He still wants to help, protect and guide him out of his challenging situations. The only way God can involve Himself in an individual's life is if that person gives Him access.

In the following chapter, we will explore the life of Joseph, a man who really had no reason to hope in the future, yet because of a promise that God made to him in a dream, he was able to overcome betrayal by family members and other people close to him. When his inner circle of influence collapsed, it was God's vow that fueled his desire to win big. Joseph's victory was so complete in the end that he was not only able to make a better life for himself, but he helped to spare an entire nation from destruction due to a severe famine. Like Joseph, your life is a success story waiting to happen and be told!

It Starts With a Vision

2

It Starts With a Vision

*"And the Lord answered me and said, Write the vision and engrave it
so plainly upon tablets that everyone who passes may [be able to]
read [it easily and quickly] as he hastens by"*
(Habakkuk 2:2, *The Amplified Bible*).

Even before an athlete has tied his shoelaces, he knows that he
must imagine himself crossing the finish line in order to win. He
knows that if he can't see himself as a winner, he will never
succeed. A vision is what keeps him going during the long
months of training. It is what gets him out of bed well before the
sun has risen each morning and before most people have begun
to stir. And when the day of the race has finally come, it is what
keeps him going when his muscles are cramping, his feet are
blistered and his legs feel like they are going to give out. A vision
is what takes him across the finish line. Without a doubt, I can
boldly declare that **vision is your launching pad to your
future**.

I think that long distance running is the most difficult of all
track competitions. An athlete has to maintain his stamina and
keep pushing, even when he wants to quit mentally and
physically. Life is a lot like a long distance race. We start out
with enthusiasm for the future and an assurance that we will be

successful in whatever we do. Then things begin to happen that slow us down. It might be a financial crisis, like losing a job or an unexpected household or car repair, or a serious medical condition that just knocks the wind out of us. But no matter what the devil throws our way to get us to quit, we must pick ourselves up and keep running.

An example of a biblical personality who was a good long distance runner is Joseph of the Old Testament. Throughout this book I will mention of his life and triumph over adversity. I believe that his life is a testimonial of what happens when you adapt a winner's mentality.

Once Joseph received the vision from God about his life, he did not allow anything to sway him from his destiny. Through his life experiences, we see what it takes to endure any adversity we might encounter on our way to fulfilling our vision.

Joseph was Jacob's eleventh son. Jacob's wife, Rebekah, had been barren for many years before she was finally able to bare her husband a son in his old age. Jacob loved Joseph more than any of his other children and constantly favored him throughout his life. He even had a special coat of many colors made for his favorite son. Early on, Joseph's brothers envied his favored position in the family.

Joseph was a 17-year old young man when he received a glimpse of his future. One night he dreamt that his brothers bowed down and served him. A short time later, he had another dream where his parents also bowed down to him (Genesis 37:5-9). He was excited about his future, but found that when he told his family about his destiny, they weren't as excited. They didn't see the big picture. His brothers only saw a young, smart aleck kid bossing them around. Their jealously then escalated to the point where they plotted to murder him.

God, however, had another plan. It was vital for the future of His chosen people that Joseph's vision be fulfilled. After his brothers threw Joseph in a pit, they noticed a band of Egyptian slave traders making their way across the desert. Upon seeing the caravan, the brothers decided to make a profit on their brother by selling him into slavery and avoid having to cover up his murder (Genesis 37:12-28). In Egypt Joseph was sold to Potiphar, an official who served Pharaoh as captain of the guard.

Regardless of the evil plans of his brothers, it was imperative that Joseph reach his destiny. His dreams were God-ordained. They were given to him so that he would have something to hold on to during his 13-year odyssey of hope and despair. Deuteronomy 29:29 says, *"The secret things belong unto the Lord our God: but those things which are revealed belong unto us and to our children for ever, that we may do all the words of this law."* We must realize that when God shows us the secret things, it's not always just for us. It's usually for others as well. In this case, Joseph's vision wasn't about him bossing around his brothers. It was about saving an entire nation.

> **"A VISION IS YOUR LAUNCHING PAD TO YOUR FUTURE."**

What exactly is vision? A *vision* is "a redemptive revelation of the purpose of God for you and others." A vision allows you to see what God sees. Joseph's vision enabled him to endure many long years in Egyptian slavery and prison. Because of it, he was able to hold on to what he received from God and never give up on it coming to pass.

Proverbs 29:18 says, *"Where there is no vision, the people perish...."* The word *perish* in this verse means, "to be made naked." In other words, a person without a vision is stripped and exposed to shame and open to danger. Joseph's vision helped him to overcome the hardships he experienced. It set the direction for his life and enabled him to rise to the head of Potiphar's household. When he was later falsely accused of attempted rape by Potiphar's wife and subsequently thrown into prison, he was not bound with shame but was eventually elevated to the head of the prison. In some ways, Joseph was similar to an athlete who was pressured to quit, but didn't despite the opposition. He never lost sight of his future victory.

An athlete who loses his vision, loses his value, or worth. He becomes complacent, idle and doesn't have the passion to continue training, let alone compete. When it's time to get up early and run, he rolls over in bed and hits the snooze button on the alarm clock. His body is screaming, I'm tired and sore, and he willingly obliges to it. When he thinks about bringing home the "gold," he easily talks himself out of it as he dwells on the superiority of his competition. If he pulls a hamstring or tears a knee tendon, instead of undergoing intense physical therapy, he abandons his goals and throws in the towel. Clearly, his lack of vision is his downfall.

Now pay attention to this statement: **Vision doesn't perish without people, but people will perish without a vision. You see, *someone* will win the prize. If you give up on your dreams, it just won't be you.** If you don't have a vision, you won't know where you are headed; and you won't have anything to strive toward. I've often said, "If you don't know where you're going, how will you know when you get there?" You see, vision gives you a benchmark to strive for, and it causes you to be more focused.

All too often, we focus on our present circumstances and that's the only thing we see. We get so caught up in our little world and our little problems that we don't see anything else. We don't look beyond our circumstances and into our future to see what God sees. When you know what God's plan for your life is, you will press through any distraction or hardship you encounter until you reach your final destination.

You'll also look at your situation differently. Instead of feeling like your circumstances will never change, you'll stop feeling helpless and take whatever steps are necessary to turn your situation around. Having a vision helps you to overcome the mistakes of your past. It will help you to realize that your past is over and that you don't need to be in bondage to it. You'll realize that where you are now doesn't have to be your final stopping point. Vision gives you hope for a better future and the courage to walk toward a greater tomorrow.

Keep Your Eyes on the Prize

As you run your long-distance race to win the prize of seeing the manifestation of your vision, you'll encounter many outside forces from well-meaning friends, family and associates who will, with all good intentions, work against your vision. In an effort to try to get you to be "realistic" (so they say) about your situation, they will try to give you advice that will only cause you to doubt what God has spoken to you. When this happens, you must maintain your focus on the desired end result. Only then will you be able to endure any hardships you encounter and any frustration that you feel. Realize that when you keep your eyes on your vision, you will be infused with a continual supply of supernatural energy. Likewise, when you focus on the hardships and on your frustrations, you will begin to sink.

This is what happened to Peter when he walked on the water. After Jesus sent His disciples to go ahead of Him, Jesus went up on a mountainside to pray. Later that night, the disciples were in their boat a considerable distance from shore. They were having a hard time reaching the shore because the wind was blowing against them and the boat was being tossed by the huge waves. In the middle of the night, they saw Jesus walking on the water. At Jesus' request, Peter jumped out of the boat and began to walk on the water. He successfully took a few steps but became distracted because of the wind and the waves. When he took his eyes off of Jesus, he began to sink (Matthew 14:22-32).

Life can sometimes make you feel as though you are struggling to reach your destination and everything seems to be against you. For example, your company lost a huge contract, and your boss blames you. Your child, who was once sweet and obedient, turned rebellious, and you get a call on your job that she has been expelled from school. Perhaps you've had the same job for 20 years and suddenly get laid off, or you decide to start your own business but things aren't going as planned. You are trying to reach land, but the winds and the waves of life are battering your ship.

We see in Matthew 14 that Peter's downfall happened when he stopped looking at Jesus—his answer to life's challenges. Jesus' life and victories are symbolic of our vision. So, when we keep our eyes on Him, we can succeed at anything.

When you receive a vision from God, you also receive four things that will help you obtain the vision. They are **motivation, evaluation, transformation** and **dedication**. Let's take a closer look at each of these things.

First, vision produces *motivation* because it enables you to believe that you can do the impossible. God often asks us to do things we have never done before. He may want you to step out in ministry, start a business, write a book or produce a movie.

The list can be endless. Vision gives you the confidence to believe that you can accomplish anything you set your hand to do, even if you don't have any experience in that area.

Secondly, to achieve your vision, you must *evaluate*, or examine yourself. After careful evaluation, you can determine what areas you need to sharpen to help you obtain your goal. Do you need to get training in a particular area? What knowledge do you need to be successful? During this stage, you should also evaluate the direction you are taking as well as seek advice from people who are knowledgeable about what you want to do.

Thirdly, *transformation* takes place as you walk out your destiny. Transformation is the ability to change or adapt. Joseph learned how to successfully adapt in every situation he found himself in. He went from favored son, to slave, to household manager, to prisoner, to head of the prisoners, and to second in command in Egypt. Throughout the many ups and downs in his life, he always landed on his feet because his trust in God enabled him to adapt and make the best of each situation.

On your way to fulfilling your dreams, you may find yourself doing things that you had never dreamed of. You may be the analytical type but now have to be more creative to get the word out about your vision. You may have never wanted to speak publicly before, but in order to achieve your goal, you are now speaking to business leaders, government officials and even to the media.

Finally, vision produces *dedication*. As long as you hold your dream before your eyes, you will be loyal to its completion rather than dropping it because of adversity or getting sidetracked by something else that comes along that seems easier. Vision keeps you focused on your task at hand.

Helen Keller was a popular American author of the 19th and

20th Century who lost her sight and hearing due to meningitis when she was 19 months old. She was once asked, "What is worse than being blind?" She replied, "Having sight without vision." Although she had no control over how she became blind, she did have an impact on how she left this world. When her tutor, Anne Sullivan, came into her life at age seven and taught her sign language, her life was transformed. She eventually graduated from Radcliffe College, learned to read French, German, Greek and Latin in Braille, traveled to 39 countries, met 12 U.S. Presidents and authored 14 books. Although Helen didn't have physical sight, she had a vision; and she would not allow anything to stop her from fulfilling that vision.

What an inspiration she is to those of us who can see. She ran her race in life well. All too often, those of us who can see allow our *sight* to hinder our *vision*. In the middle of a trying situation, we might have to close our eyes to what is going on around us so we can focus on what is on the inside of us; and like Helen Keller, achieve the impossible.

Vision's Adversity

Earlier in this chapter, I gave you my definition of the word *vision*, which is "a redemptive revelation of the purpose of God for your life and for the lives of others." Redemption implies that the vision is not just for you but for others as well. The word *revelation* here means "illumination, or enlightenment and understanding." In other words, you can clearly visualize it. The light bulb has turned on. Now, it's important to realize that after you "see it," you *will* experience a period of affliction. Hebrews 10:32, AMP says, *"But be ever mindful of the days gone by in which, after you were first spiritually enlightened, you endured a great and painful struggle."*

This happens because the Devil does not want you to receive anything from God, and will do anything to get you to back off from what God has spoken to your heart. If he can get you to change your mind, he will not only affect your life but the lives of the people you encounter as well. However, if you stay on course, you will be able to pull many people out of Satan's control and from his kingdom of darkness, and bring them on over to God's side into the kingdom of light.

Don't be surprised when adversity comes. You will experience what I call "internal" and "external" pressures. External pressures come from people you encounter on a daily basis but you don't really know them. In the course of doing business, you might have a hard time with the bank teller or the postal clerk. You might even get into an argument with the postman. It's really someone you encounter who is having a bad day and is passing his or her frustration on to you.

Internal pressures, on the other hand, come from people who are close to you. They make up your "inner circle" of friends. These are the people you trust, and you feel that you can speak to them in confidence. In looking at Joseph's life, he first received pressure from his brothers. They weren't at all open to what he had to say (Genesis 37:8-11). In fact, after sharing the vision with his brothers, Genesis 37:5 says that his brothers hated him.

The same thing may happen to you. Your close friends and family may hate you because you received the vision and they didn't. If this happens, realize that they are simply acting selfishly and are not walking in accordance with God's commandment of love (Luke 10:28). Like Joseph's family, they don't see the big picture. They don't realize that God has given you this vision to strategically place you in a position where you will be able to grab their hands so that they will be nourished and one day be able to live life in abundance. It's up to you, therefore, to take the higher road and continually walk in love toward them by ignoring their unkind remarks.

Keep in mind that some people won't be able to handle what God shows you. Jesus gave us wise advice in Matthew 7:6 when He said, *"Give not that which is holy unto the dogs, neither cast ye your pearls before swine, lest they trample them under their feet, and turn again and rend you."* So be wise enough to recognize this and wait until the appropriate time to share your vision.

Don't be too quick to share your vision with others. It can help to alleviate a lot of potential hardships.

> "A VISION CAN FEEL SO BIG ON THE INSIDE OF YOU THAT YOU FEEL AS THOUGH YOU ARE GOING TO BURST."

Walking Out the Vision

In chapter one, I listed the different stages of becoming a competitive runner. You have to start out slow and build yourself up to long distance running and marathons. No one starts out at these levels. However, every long distance and marathon runner began with a vision. This is because the vision gives the runner a starting point. Your vision is your starting point.

When you receive a vision from the Lord, it's important to pray about what He has spoken to your heart. You want to make sure that you have heard *His* voice and not your own. When you are sure that God has spoken to you, you want to clearly understand what He is telling you to do. This will keep you on the right path.

After you have received your vision, then it's necessary to establish a plan. This is an outline, or the steps you need to take to accomplish your goals. Habakkuk 2:2 says, *"...Write the vision,*

and make it plain upon tables, that he may run that readeth it."
You've heard the saying, "We need to plan our work and then
work our plan." This is a crucial step in reaching your destiny.
Many people get off their designated path because they never
took the time to write down a plan. They either keep getting
sidetracked or lost along the way. Writing down a plan and
sticking to it will guarantee that you reach your desired
destination.

Finally, timing is important. You might have a great vision,
but some things need to happen in your personal life before you
step out on your idea. This might include getting out of debt,
saving money or waiting until your spouse is in agreement with
your plan. Habakkuk 2:3 continues *"...the vision is yet for an
appointed time, but at the end it shall speak, and not lie: though
it tarry, wait for it; because it will surely come, it will not tarry."*
Timing can be a frustrating part of the process. A vision can
feel so big on the inside of you that you feel as though you are
going to burst. But yet, it seems as though every door around you
is closed and that people only chuckle when you talk about your
dream. To them, it's only a pipe dream. I can assure you, that if
you will be faithful and never give up on your dream, your vision
will come to pass.

You might be surprised to know that God gave me the vision
to author a book five years ago. At that time, I didn't have any
idea of what the book should be about. Three years had passed
when I began to teach our congregation about the life of Joseph
and how he overcame every pressure in life that he encountered.
At that time, I realized that the book should be about Joseph's
life. Then, even more time passed before I partnered with a
publisher. During those five years, a lot was going on in my life. I
experienced family, financial and health challenges. It would

have been very easy to quit at any time during the process. I was like Joseph and did not realize what I would go through before this project would be completed. It was through much endurance, prayer and fasting that the vision of authoring a book finally came to pass.

Receiving the Promise

Never forget that vision is a process. It's not something that happens automatically but has to happen in phases. These four phases are: 1) revelation, 2) preparation, 3) manifestation and 4) elevation. You first must receive the revelation of what God wants you to do. Then you must make the necessary preparation to accomplish your goals. After that, you must wait patiently for the manifestation of the vision. When the manifestation of your vision arrives, elevation comes. I was elevated to book author. Whatever our visions are, when they are accomplished, we are all elevated to the position of victors. Keep in mind that a period of time has to pass between each phase and that all phases are sequential. In other words, you can't skip over step two to quickly reach step four, and you can't get started if you never receive step one, a revelation.

During each phase, you will experience pressure, challenges, trials and hardships. There is no way to escape adversity; however, you have God's Word that you will overcome it. You can liken the challenges you encounter as the training a runner endures to get his body in shape. I don't think any athlete really "likes" the pain he experiences when training. However, he pushes himself to build his endurance and keeps at it because he wants to win the race. The same is true for you. You need to keep at it until you see your vision come into reality. You can quit anytime along the journey, but if you do, you won't win the prize.

Therefore, be encouraged and keep reminding yourself of what the Bible says in Habakkuk 2:3. Your vision *will* one day speak if you wait for it.

We are encouraged to *"Cast not away therefore your confidence, which has great recompense of reward"* (Hebrews 10:35). As you are waiting for the fulfillment of your vision, never forget that God always causes you to triumph (2 Corinthians 2:14). He has also declared that we are more than conquerors through Christ Jesus.

The Apostle Paul experienced a lot of persecution during his ministry. Yet, he boldly proclaimed, *"If God be for us, who can be against us?"* (Romans 8:31). He went on to say, *"Who shall separate us from the love of Christ? Shall trouble or hardship or persecution or famine or nakedness or danger or sword? As it is written: 'For your sake we face death all day long; we are considered as sheep to be slaughtered.' No, in all these things we are more than conquerors through him who loved us"* vv. 35-37, *NIV*. Regardless of what you encounter, God has made a way for you to be successful in reaching your vision.

In addition to the Word of God, you have been given the ability to pray the mysteries of God by praying in other tongues. (Romans 8:26-27.) When you don't know what to do in a situation, you can tap into the very mind of God when praying in the Spirit. Rest assured, God has given you everything you need to see your vision come to pass.

Be encouraged by our biblical example of a long-distance runner. Joseph didn't realize everything he would encounter after he had the two dreams about his future. He was just excited that one day he was going to rule over his family. He had no idea that he would be thrown in a pit, sold into slavery, sentenced to prison and finally become second in command to Pharaoh. A period of 13 years passed from the time he received the vision and the fulfillment of that vision. However, he never lost hope in God's promise to him. He kept his vision intact, and God promoted him in every situation he was in.

Connecting With Your Personal Trainer

3

3

Connecting With Your Personal Trainer

"And thou shalt love the Lord thy God with all thine heart, and with all thy soul, and with all thy might" (Deuteronomy 6:5).

You may or may not be a sports enthusiast, but if you are familiar with athletics, you know that it takes persistence, commitment and a refusal to quit in order to be a successful athlete. Hours of training and practice are the keys to developing the strength and endurance needed to win when it comes time to run the race.

The professional athlete will inevitably find him or herself pitted against some pretty fierce competition, and it will take more than fancy footwork to come out on top. The mindset of the athlete will make the difference in who will cross the finish line first, score the winning touchdown, or make the goal that will propel the team to victory. When the pressure is on, only the strongest players cross the finish line and win the prize.

The same is true where the Christian's life is concerned. Often, the track field of life is filled with Believers who haven't decided that they will stand in the midst of adversity and refuse to give up when the pressure is on. As a result, they live consistently defeated lives, never really walking in the authority and power that God has designed for them to walk.

Have you been there? I know I have. When I gave birth to my first child, I experienced some serious health challenges that threatened my life. I was taken to the emergency room, barely able to breathe and with abnormally high blood pressure. The doctors diagnosed me with congestive heart failure. Talk about adversity and pressure.

I knew it was an attack from Satan against my body because I had just given birth to my son and the Devil was trying to snatch my life. I refused, however, to buckle under the pressure. I stood firm on the Word of God by confessing Scripture verses, knowing that I was healed in spite of the doctor's bad report. Eventually, my healing manifested. I refused to cave in and quit when I knew that I had a right to divine health. You can say that I connected with my spiritual "Personal Trainer"—God; and as a result of putting Him and His Word first in my life, everything turned around.

Just like the track runner who feels like he just doesn't have the energy to sprint the last leg of the relay, we all have experienced moments of intense pressure when it seemed like we didn't have what it took to win the race of life. The good news is that God has equipped you with the tools necessary to win your race and claim your prize. He has given you His Word and the Holy Spirit. But it's up to you to maximize what He has put in your hands and in your spirit in order to obtain victory under pressure.

Joseph: A Winner Against All Odds

Becoming victorious in the midst of adversity is a trademark of those individuals who trust God. Take Joseph for example. He is one of the greatest faith champions in the Bible. His faith was challenged every step of the way as God led him to his destiny.

This was a man who faced incredible odds and adversity and still came out on top. That's because Joseph was committed to the vision God had placed in his heart and he refused to let his circumstances dictate his progress and performance. As a result of his tenacity and consistency in his walk with God, he became the second in command in all of Egypt.

The deck of cards was stacked against Joseph from day one. His brothers hated him because he was their father's favorite child, and they envied the fact that God regularly spoke to him in dreams and visions. In fact, they were jealous of him to such an extent that they conspired to kill him, and they almost got away with it. Think of that!

I don't know whether you have experienced that type of persecution from your own family members, but imagine how Joseph felt; his own flesh and blood threw him in a pit and left him to die (Genesis 37). They thought that was the end of the story, but God had another plan. Though it seemed like Joseph's life was over, God's perfect will was still in motion; however, it would take Joseph's faith to bring it to pass.

Genesis 39:1-6 describes Joseph's journey from the pit to the palace of the pharaoh of Egypt. It says:

> *And Joseph was brought down to Egypt; and Potiphar, an officer of Pharaoh, captain of the guard, an Egyptian, bought him of the hands of the Ishmaelites, which had brought him down thither. And the Lord was with Joseph, and he was a prosperous man; and he was in the house of his master the Egyptian. And his master saw that the Lord was with him, and that the Lord made all that he did to prosper in his hand. And Joseph found grace in his sight, and he served him: and he made him overseer over his house, and all that he had he put into his hand. And it came to pass from the time*

> *that he had made him overseer in his house, and*
> *over all that he had, that the Lord blessed the*
> *Egyptian's house for Joseph's sake; and the blessing*
> *of the Lord was upon all that he had in the house,*
> *and in the field. And he left all that he had in*
> *Joseph's hand; and he knew not aught he had, save*
> *the bread which he did eat. And Joseph was a*
> *goodly person, and well favored.*

I find that one of the most interesting things about what happened to Joseph was that even though he was a slave, the Scripture says that he *prospered*. He went from one bad situation to another; but, in the midst of it all, the blessing of God was still on his life. Why? I believe there are a number of reasons.

First, **Joseph made God his first priority**. He was committed to his relationship with the heavenly Father and he had a clear understanding of his covenant with Him. As a result, he was able to stay focused on his victory in the midst of adversity. Joseph was like many Christians today who find themselves in troubling circumstances even though God has given them a clear vision for their futures. **The difference between those who are winners and those who are not is the type of personal relationship they have with God.**

A *priority* is defined as "that which is of first importance." Your priorities in life are those things that are at the top of your "to-do" list. The question you must ask yourself is, *Is there anything in my life that has taken priority over my relationship with God?* It could be your job, a relationship or even an activity that you love to do. If you do find that your priorities are out of line, it is time to refocus your attention on what should be your *first* priority, and that is establishing a close relationship with the Father.

If you are not sure exactly how to do that, Matthew 6:33 gives some clear direction on one of the key ways to establishing an intimate relationship with God. It says, *"But seek ye first the kingdom of God, and his righteousness; and all these things shall be added unto you."* What this means is that you have to make God's kingdom, or His way of doing things, your first priority in life. When you do that, everything else, including the blessing of God, will be added to your life. Just like Joseph, when your relationship with God is your first priority, and pleasing Him is your prime focus, especially in the face of trouble, success is inevitable.

Just because you find yourself in a challenging situation, your relationship with God shouldn't be adversely affected. In fact, being in the "fiery furnace" should only help to refine and strengthen your relationship with Him because it forces you to trust Him even more. Life's adversities should be your stepping-stones to getting closer to God and not farther away from Him. Having a personal relationship with Jesus will cause you to triumph because it is only through Him that victory is possible.

> "THE DIFFERENCE BETWEEN THOSE WHO ARE WINNERS AND THOSE WHO ARE NOT IS THE TYPE OF PERSONAL RELATIONSHIP THEY HAVE WITH GOD."

Deuteronomy 6:5 commands us to *"...love the Lord thy God with all thine heart, and with all thy soul, and with all thy might."* This is the first and great commandment. When you look at Joseph's life, it is apparent that he had true fellowship with God; he loved Him. It is critical that every Believer diligently cultivate a love relationship with God. I believe that Joseph mastered his love walk and truly loved the Lord with all his heart, soul, mind and strength. Even when his brothers demonstrated their hatred toward him by trying to kill him, he continued to walk in love toward them. Joseph surrendered his life to God completely and I know that is the reason why God made things happen for him time and time again. The Lord was his first priority.

I believe that when we make God our first priority, we can also experience the supernatural favor of God on our lives. This comes through spending quality time with Him in His Word until it consumes us. It also means consulting Him before making any decisions. Again, it is a matter of priority. By walking in love toward others, we demonstrate our love for the Father. When faith and confidence rise within us, God is able to get us out of any situation in which we find ourselves.

Look Straight Ahead

One of the primary tools that the enemy uses against Christians is *distractions*. He knows that if he can get your eyes off of God and on your problems, cares and concerns, you will be drawn away from reaching your life's goals. Distractions come to invade our minds to bring us to a state of confusion. They can come in many forms, but their objective is the same every time— to get your focus off of God. You can see why building a solid relationship with Him is so vital, because it allows you to have a mentality that refuses to give up in the midst of turmoil. When the foundation of your relationship with God is secure, you won't let distractions pull you away from your devotion to the Lord.

First Corinthians 7:35, *The Amplified Bible* says, *"Now I say this for your own welfare and profit, not to put [a halter of] restraint upon you, but to promote what is seemly and in good order and to secure your undistracted and undivided devotion to the Lord."* God's desire is that your devotion to Him be free from distractions, but it is up to you to maintain this type of steadfastness for Him.

Focus and discipline are character traits that *you* are responsible for cultivating. Fear, mistreatment, temptation and adverse circumstances are all distractions that can pull you away from your focus on God and His love for you. When you make up your mind to refuse to give in to distractions, you will be able to bounce back from any setback.

Joseph never retaliated or tried to argue against his mistreatment. He was able to continue to walk in faith because his eyes remained fixed on God. You can do the same if you give Him first place in your life and refuse to get sidetracked. You have to stay focused on God.

Don't Take the Bait!

So many times distractions come in the form of temptations. Again, you can look at Joseph's experience in Potiphar's house as a reference for how and why to avoid the traps that Satan sets for you.

Joseph was the overseer of Potiphar's house, and the Scripture says that he was a very attractive man. His position of authority and physical attractiveness caught Potiphar's wife's attention, and she attempted to seduce him. Genesis 39:7 says, *"And it came to pass after these things, that his master's wife cast her eyes upon Joseph; and she said, Lie with me."* Joseph's character and commitment to God were of such quality that he responded to her advances with a question: "How could I commit such wickedness against God?"

This man of God would neither commit adultery nor betray his master's trust for a moment of temporary pleasure. That may not have been an easy decision for him, but his love for God overrode his flesh, and the Bible says he fled after being pursued by this woman day after day (Genesis 39:12). For Joseph to have given in to such a temptation would have caused him to deviate from the course God had planned for his life.

Too often, people want to blame God for tempting them, but God isn't the tempter. James 1:14-15 says, *"But every man is tempted, when he is drawn away of his own lust, and enticed. Then when lust hath conceived, it bringeth forth sin: and sin, when it is finished bringeth forth death."*

The Bible clearly says that people are drawn away because of their *own* lust, or the evil desires that are already in their hearts. That takes the responsibility off of God. While Satan can orchestrate situations in which you can potentially fall, you are the one responsible for choosing whether or not to take his bait.

Joseph refused to be drawn away by the enemy, which indicates to me that lust wasn't in his heart. He didn't bother playing around with the temptation to sin, and didn't give himself any room to compromise or to be persuaded by Potiphar's wife. That's the kind of holy dedication God is looking for in His children.

How many Christians are willing to flee the temptation to sin because of their love for God and respect for His position in their lives? Many people think that living a sin-free lifestyle is too difficult, and that it is impossible to resist temptation when it is thrown in your face, but Joseph's life proves that isn't the case. It simply depends on where you place your priorities. When you love God with all your heart, soul, mind and strength, it isn't all that difficult to turn away from sin. You simply value your relationship with Him too much to jeopardize it and risk forfeiting the blessing of God on your life.

There is no room for compromise in the life of a Believer.

Second Timothy 2:19 says, *"Nevertheless the foundation of God standeth sure, having this seal, The Lord knoweth them that are his. And, Let every one that nameth the name of Christ depart from iniquity."* God commands those who profess to be Christians to leave sin alone. It's just that simple. So why wouldn't you want to? Romans 6:23 says, *"For the wages of sin is death…"* In simple terms, sin has high consequences. The Devil's goal is to destroy your life, and when you refuse to get rid of the sin in your life, death is inevitable. It might not happen right away, but it will happen. You can't play with fire and expect not to be burned.

God doesn't give the command not to sin because He's trying to stop you from having fun; He loves you. But He knows that living a life of compromise and dabbling with sin will keep you from experiencing victory under pressure. You can't win over the Devil when you're playing around in his camp. In fact, when you're in his territory, he has a right to destroy you.

Sin will hinder your relationship with God and stop your faith from working. That's why the apostle Paul tells us to "…*lay aside every weight, and the sin which doth so easily beset us, and let us run with patience the race that is set before us*" (Hebrews 12:1). A *weight* is anything that will hinder you in the Christian race, just like ankle weights are hindrances to the speed, endurance and precision of a track runner.

Most of the time "weights" are sins, or things that lead to sin such as negative attitudes, ideas, habits, people and relationships. You have to determine those things that are "weights" in your life and make a quality decision to lay them aside.

Trusting God as Your Source

One of the most important keys to victory in the life of a

Christian is learning to trust God; He is your only Source. Joseph recognized where his abilities came from and was able to do some interesting things as a result. Read Genesis 40:1-8:

> *And it came to pass after these things, that the butler of the king of Egypt and his baker had offended their lord the king of Egypt. And Pharaoh was wroth against two of his officers, against the chief of the butlers, and against the chief of the bakers. And he put them in ward in the house of the captain of the guard, into the prison, the place where Joseph was bound. And the captain of the guard charged Joseph with them, and he served them: and they continued a season in ward. And they dreamed a dream both of them, each man his dream in one night, each man according to the interpretation of his dream, the butler and the baker of the king of Egypt, which were bound in the prison. And Joseph came in unto them in the morning, and looked upon them, and, behold, they were sad. And he asked Pharaoh's officers that were with him in the ward of his lord's house, saying, Wherefore look ye so sadly today? And they said unto him, We have dreamed a dream, and there is no interpreter of it. And Joseph said unto them, Do not interpretations belong to God? Tell me them, I pray you.*

"THERE IS NO ROOM FOR COMPROMISE IN THE LIFE OF A BELIEVER."

Joseph knew that his relationship with God was the key to his victory. Joseph would not take any credit for interpreting his dreams; he recognized that he was only a vessel to be used by the Lord. His confidence was in God, not man.

Like Joseph, you need to understand that it is only through

the power of God working in and through you that you are able to do anything. When you trust Him as your source of wisdom, understanding, blessing, ability, finances and everything else that you have in life, you are strengthened. You don't have to put yourself in God's position and try to make things happen in your own strength when you acknowledge Him as the head of your life. That takes a lot of pressure off of you, and that's how God wants it!

When you trust God, it means that you lean on Him and are confident in His ability to take care of every aspect of your life. The Bible instructs you to live your life fully trusting God every step of the way (Proverbs 3:5-6). If you recognize and acknowledge the Lord in everything you do, you can rest assured that your outcome will be good.

Just like the personal trainer who is responsible for getting the athlete into competition shape, God wants to get you into the best spiritual shape ever! He has plenty of expertise and knows just what you need to win in the game of life. As your personal Life Coach, He is quite capable of leading you down the right path; but first you must turn the controls of your life over to Him. That is what real trust is all about.

You can experience victory under pressure if you let the principles of God's Word become your foundation. Maintaining a strong relationship with Him through intimate fellowship in prayer and His Word are essential for victory. That is why you must stop living in sin, refuse to succumb to temptation, and trust Him at all cost. Regardless of the situation in which you find yourself, God has already equipped you to triumph in Christ. The price has been paid. Therefore, are you willing to stand on the Word in the midst of adversity and see the end of your faith? If so, your success in the race of life is assured!

Faithful to the
Finish

4

4

Faithful to the Finish

"Moreover it is required in stewards, that a man be found faithful"
(1 Corinthians 4:2).

George Foreman, a former heavyweight boxing champion, once said, "I am a winner each and every time I go into the ring." His heart and attitude were that of a champion, and that's what led him to victories in the boxing ring. In 1968, he was the Olympic heavyweight gold medallist, and in 1973 he received the world heavyweight crown. Although he retired from boxing in 1977 shortly after losing his title to Muhammad Ali, Foreman launched a remarkable comeback in 1987. By 1994, Foreman recaptured the heavyweight title and became the oldest heavyweight champion in boxing history. There is a notable moral behind the story of George Foreman's memorable comeback: **never give up the hope of being a champion even after you've experienced defeat!**

Perhaps you may have heard the statement, "It's not how you start, it's how you finish." Not only can George Foreman's story and this statement apply to your personal dreams, goals and aspirations, it is also true when it comes to running the Christian race. It's one thing to start off strong in faith and courage, and quite another to finish strong.

Unfortunately, many Believers have challenges when it comes to remaining faithful and sticking to what God has called them to do, especially in the midst of trials and tribulations. If they could adapt the attitude and mindset of a champion, they would see their dreams come to pass. Joseph of the Old Testament enjoyed the victory because he refused to compromise his values, even when the pressure was on. He understood the importance of faithfulness, and he reaped a great reward because of it.

> "Never give up the hope of being a champion even after you've experienced defeat!"

Like Joseph, everyone has experienced some adversity. Whether you were lied about, betrayed or mistreated in some way, I'm sure you can relate to what it feels like to be persecuted. Regardless of what you have been through, or are going through now, be encouraged by knowing that just as Joseph prospered in the midst of adversity, so can you. The key is *faithfulness*.

Staying the Course

There are stages that you will go through on the way to seeing the vision of God come to pass in your life, so get ready. When He has a plan for you, you will make several pit stops on the way to your final destination. The good news is that with every stop you make, you will experience another level of growth and promotion if you are determined to stay the course. The attitude you take with you as you travel along life's roads will determine your success. **Poor attitude equals poor success. Good attitude equals good success.**

I believe that Joseph's success was a result of his understanding what true faithfulness is. He was able to go through some pretty uncomfortable situations and still keep his head up. The Scriptures repeatedly tell us that the Lord was with him. What does that mean? God was there to guide and protect him every step of the way.

No matter what situation Joseph was in, nothing could hold this man of God down or keep him stuck in one place. He was constantly being promoted and everything he did prospered. Some people would say that he had the "Midas touch." But as Christians we know that God's limitless blessings were upon Joseph.

Remaining faithful to God is critical to you seeing the end of your faith as well. So, what does it mean to be *faithful*? When you are faithful, you are strict and thorough in the performance of your duties regardless of what is going on around you. It also means that you are steady in allegiance or affection, loyal, reliable, devoted and trustworthy. In sum, to be faithful means that you do what you are supposed to do all the time, no matter what. That may seem like a lot to ask, but God is holding every Christian to this standard. He is looking for faithfulness in the lives of His children.

Psalm 31:23 says this: *"O love the Lord, all ye his saints: for the Lord preserveth the faithful, and plentifully rewardeth the proud doer."* The Word of God clearly lets us know that God Himself is faithful to those who choose to be faithful. To *preserve* means "to keep, protect or sustain." God keeps, protects, sustains and preserves people who are reliable, trustworthy and devoted to His plans, purposes and pursuits. When you are faithful to seek His way of doing things in every situation, maintaining your allegiance to Him even in the face of compromise, He will make good on His promises to keep and protect you.

That's what happened in Joseph's life. Even though he had the opportunity to sin with Potiphar's wife, he kept his eyes on his relationship with God. He was faithful to his commitment to God and wasn't willing to sacrifice his relationship with the Father for the temporary pleasure of sin. Joseph was faithful, trustworthy and devoted to God, and therefore experienced continual protection, preservation and prosperity. As you remain faithful to God, you can experience the same benefits.

Settle It

You may want to go to the next level that God has for you in life, but if you haven't settled the faithfulness issue, you simply won't see the results of your faith. Whether you realize it or not, there are consequences for not being faithful to God. First of all, you set yourself up to miss out on what He intends for you to have. The Word of God tells us that a faithful man abounds in blessings (Proverbs 28:20). In other words, things will continually go well for him in every area of his life. To refuse to live a lifestyle of faithfulness is asking for trouble. You won't be a candidate for promotion and increase.

God's empowerment on your life is a result of your quality decision to be faithful to Him. It's not enough just to say that you are faithful; it has to be a lifestyle. Attending church every Sunday doesn't necessarily mean you are faithful to God. He is looking at your personal relationship with Him when you aren't in front of other people.

Are you faithful to walk in love and consistently seek God's way of doing things in *every* situation you face? He knows that you will make mistakes, but your faithfulness is demonstrated in your allegiance to Him even when the going gets tough. When the Devil is throwing his hardest punches, are you willing to stand on the Word of God, or does doubt, wavering and unbelief take over your thinking and speech? Will the pressure get the best of you? These are the areas that you need to examine in your life. You may find that you haven't been as faithful as you thought you were.

It's the Little Things That Count

Sometimes people get off track because they think God is looking at some major milestone they reached in their walk with Him, or some great deed they did. Honestly, He is looking at your faithfulness in the little things. That's what counts in the long run. Again, in the race of life, how you finish makes all the difference.

Diligence and consistency in tending to your responsibilities are what make you a candidate for promotion. You are a steward over the time, resources and assignments that God has given you. So, what are you doing with what is already in your hands? You may want to be a millionaire, but how faithful have you been with your current salary? How loyal are you to your employer? Do you report to work on time? Do you spend an extra 5 or 10 minutes during your break time? It makes you wonder.

First Corinthians 4:2 says, "*Moreover it is required in stewards, that a man be found faithful.*" *The Amplified Bible* says that a faithful man proves himself worthy of trust. This verse lets us know that it is essential for a steward, or one who has been given responsibility over something, to be faithful. Going back to the definition of faithfulness we discussed earlier, a good steward is loyal, devoted and strict and thorough in the performance of his duties, regardless of what is going on around him.

Joseph always did what was required of him by God. As you study his life, you'll notice that he was placed in positions where he had to stay submitted to those in authority over him. Because of his reputation as being trustworthy and dependable, his masters did not have to constantly check up on him. He did what he was supposed to do, even when no one was around. As a result, he was well-favored and was eventually promoted to a position of authority.

Look at Matthew 25:21 (AMP) which says:

> *His master said to him, Well done, you upright [honorable, admirable] and faithful servant! You have been faithful and trustworthy over a little; I will put you in charge of much. Enter into and share the joy (the delight, the blessedness) which your master enjoys.*

I believe that faithfulness is a prerequisite to promotion. Just like Joseph, when you remain faithful and trustworthy over the seemingly little things in your life, God will increase your responsibility and span of influence.

Now comes the hard part, which is the charge to take a look at your own life. I'm sure you will be able to locate areas where you could be more faithful. It may be on your job, in your relationships and interactions with your family and friends, or even in the area of how you are using the gifts and talents God has given you.

Often, people want to move on to what they consider bigger opportunities, but they haven't proven themselves faithful with what they already have. This is particularly true where your finances are concerned. Everyone wants to lay claim to wealth and riches, and nothing is wrong with that. But how are you managing the finances that you already have? Are you a tither and a consistent giver? Do you pay your bills on time and save your money? Are you irresponsible with your money? The practical things are what make the difference. Before God will bless you with more, He has to see that He can trust you with what you already have.

Can your employer depend on you to utilize his time and resources wisely? Does your integrity level stay the same when no one is around? This is what it means to be faithful in the little things. God may have shown you a great vision for your life, perhaps that you would be in full-time ministry one day. But what are you doing now? How is your prayer life? Are you faithfully serving God in your local church, even if it means serving in a capacity that isn't front and center?

God is even looking at what you are doing with the knowledge and understanding you are getting from His Word. Be faithful in applying and walking in the basic truths that you already know. Luke 12:48 says, *"But he that knew not, and did commit things worthy of stripes, shall be beaten with few stripes. For unto whomsoever much is given, of him shall be much required: and to whom men have committed much, of him they will ask the more."* You won't be a candidate for greater revelation until you are faithful with the revelation you have now. Similarly, the more responsibilities you have, that much more will be required of you. The good news is that if you are determined to stay faithful, God will equip you with what it takes to do the job and do it right, whether someone is watching or not.

Faithfulness and living a disciplined life go hand in hand. It takes discipline to remain faithful, and faithfulness to achieve a standard of discipline. Most of the time, if you can find a man who is faithful, he is disciplined in other areas of his life. To *discipline* is "to train or instruct, or impose order upon something or someone." Discipline extends from the way you handle your finances to your diligence in taking care of your physical body. It means that you impose structure and order in specific areas of your life and you stick to that structure.

Just like an athlete who performs the same exercises over and over again in order to win in his or her sport, when you are disciplined, you are consistent in doing the same thing over and over again to achieve the desired results. It doesn't matter how that athlete feels, what the weather report says or what he may be going through personally. When it's time to practice, faithfulness and discipline have to kick in. You have to adopt the same attitude if you want to win in the game of life.

Perhaps you desire a promotion on your job, but are you reliable, trustworthy and loyal where you are now? God is looking at your faithfulness across the board, in every arena of life. Luke 16:10 also says that if you are faithful in the little things, you will be faithful in much. That sounds like a guarantee to me! God is saying that your proven trustworthiness where you are now will set you up for increase. He promises to elevate you to higher levels in life when you are a good steward over what you already have.

Remaining Faithful Under Pressure

One of the biggest tests of faithfulness is how you handle pressure situations. Have you ever been in a situation where the pressure from the Devil was so great that you felt you wanted to cave in and quit on God? I've been there before. Having gone through some serious health challenges and refusing to succumb to the attacks on my body, I know what it's like to stay faithful to the Word of God under pressure. I know it's not easy, but if you would settle the issue that no matter what happens, you are going to remain steadfast and immovable in the face of opposition, you *will* see victory.

Again, trace the life of Joseph. He was left for dead by his family and sold into slavery as a result. He was lied on and thrown in prison for a crime he didn't commit. But even in the midst of these types of situations, he was devoted to God; and he refused to compromise. Joseph stayed faithful wherever he found himself. He was faithful in prison and he was faithful when he was promoted to second in command over the entire land of Egypt. He didn't allow his emotions or his circumstances to tamper with his decision to stay loyal to God. Where can God send you because of your faithfulness to Him? Look again at Proverbs 28:20, "*A faithful man shall abound with blessings: but he that maketh haste to be rich shall not be innocent.*" Blessings are a by-product of faithfulness. Your steadfastness will move God's hand to get involved in your situation.

> **"YOUR PROVEN TRUSTWORTHINESS WHERE YOU ARE NOW WILL SET YOU UP FOR INCREASE."**

Protection, promotion and **provision** are three guarantees from God when you choose to remain faithful to Him. The hand of the enemy can't touch you when you make faithfulness a lifestyle. He will make sure that all of your needs are met and that you lack nothing. By setting your affection and loyalty on God at all times, you reserve a spot under His wings of protection and care. Even though storms will come, they won't have the power to move you.

I don't know about you, but those are three promises that I don't want to miss out on. Joseph abounded in blessings because of his faithfulness and so can you. When you look at his life and how he stood his ground in all the tests and trials he experienced, you can be encouraged. As long as you choose to stay faithful to God, His blessing will be on your life and you will be empowered to excel in every arena just like Joseph. You will see the end of your faith and taste the sweetness of victory, even under pressure.

Dr. Martin Luther King Jr. once said, "Faith is taking the first step even when you don't see the whole staircase." Faithfulness in pursuing the will of God for your life requires faith. Although you may not see the big picture now, trust His guidance. Don't allow fear of failure and defeat to rob you of reaching your God-ordained destiny. Remember, develop the heart and attitude of a champion and you'll win every time!

Overcoming the Unforgiveness Hurdle

5

5

Overcoming the Unforgiveness Hurdle

"And be ye kind one to another, tenderhearted, forgiving one another, even as God for Christ's sake hath forgiven you" (Ephesians 4:32).

Imagine yourself on a team of relay runners whose main event is the hurdles. Everyone on the team has the skills to win every competition you enter. Unfortunately, one of your teammates never seems to "pull his weight." In other words, he isn't doing his part to help the team succeed. He seems to always make excuses, never shows up for practice or always arrives late. And to top it off, he has an unhealthy diet. Consequently, his speed diminishes and he can't seem to clear the hurdles like he used to. It's obvious the he has to shape up or be released from the team.

Sloppy and undisciplined athletes can't win big in life. That is why athletes must keep their bodies in top condition to excel at their particular sport. That means exercising, getting enough rest and being careful to avoid eating unhealthy foods. When one area in their regimen is out of balance, it throws their whole system off and jeopardizes their performance.

The same is true in the life of a Christian. Cultivating your relationship with God is similar to the workout the athlete puts himself through in order to build his body, strength and endurance; it takes practice. In addition, making sure that you keep the wrong things out of your spirit will equip you to run your Christian race more efficiently and successfully. There is no way around doing the necessary things to get results.

Unforgiveness is one of those things that, if left unchecked, will ruin your walk with the Lord and hinder what He wants to do in your life. You simply won't experience victory if you allow it to fester in your spirit; it is like poison, or some other harmful substance that you introduce into your system. It will destroy you.

In continuing to look at Joseph's life, it is undeniable that he had the potential to let unforgiveness consume him. If he had allowed it to take control over him, he wouldn't have prospered the way that he did. I don't know too many people who could have suffered the type of treatment that Joseph endured and still have been able to walk in love. I'm sure he had his moments when he was tempted to give up, cave in and quit, but his relationship with God was too precious to him to allow that to happen. He pressed on in spite of the odds that were stacked against him.

Everywhere Joseph went, it seemed like he was getting the bad end of the deal. Time after time, he was faced with situations and circumstances that not only challenged his faith, but put him in situations where he had the potential to walk in hatred toward others. Think about it. His brothers tried to kill him out of jealousy, he was sold into slavery, falsely accused of attempted rape, and thrown in prison. If anyone had a reason to not forgive, Joseph did; but he chose to preserve his integrity by forgiving those who wronged him and allowing God to come to his aid. As a result, he experienced promotion at every turn and became the second in command over Egypt.

Forgiving others isn't easy, but it is necessary. Everyone has faced challenges where they were tempted to condemn or judge others, or stay angry and hateful towards them. But that's not how God deals with us. He is love, and we are to treat others with the love with which He loves us, no matter what they may have done to us. How willing are you to forgive those who have hurt you? Your answer will determine whether God will do the same for you.

A Clogged Spiritual Artery

Harboring unforgiveness will cause you to have a closed spirit. When this happens, you put up walls of self-protection and refuse to let God or anyone else penetrate them. Love simply can't get into your heart when you have bitterness, resentment or unforgiveness residing there.

See unforgiveness as a spiritual "artery clogger." When a person has a clogged artery, the flow of blood and oxygen from the heart to other vital organs, is hindered. As a result, a heart attack or stroke may occur, which can result in death. That's what unforgiveness does; it stops the flow of God's power in your life and cuts you off from His promises. This build up of bitterness, resentment and unforgiveness in your spirit will also strap a burden of emotional stress on your shoulders. Instead of being a carrier of the burden-removing, yoke-destroying power of God, you become a carrier of the burden! That's not the will of God. On the other hand, forgiving others gives you the opportunity to release the love of God and live the abundant life of overflowing prosperity that God has designed for your life.

Joseph was able to see beyond the wrongs he had suffered to focus on his future. Because God had already given him a glimpse into his destiny through a divinely inspired dream, he was able to move forward with confidence in the knowledge that no matter what he was going through, there was victory on the other side of the challenges he faced. He was able to let go of his past in order to get to his future. He was willing to release the past hurts and pain for the sake of a greater purpose, which was the will of God for his life. Joseph had his future on his mind and he didn't let unforgiveness stop him from reaching his goal. So likewise, in order for you to reach your final destination in life, which includes abundance, wealth, deliverance and everything else God promised you in His Word, you have to be willing to receive forgiveness from God and release it to others as well.

> "YOU CAN'T EXPECT TO HAVE YOUR PRAYERS ANSWERED WHEN YOU'RE HOLDING ON TO AUGHT AND UNFORGIVENESS."

The Scriptures are clear on this issue of forgiveness. First, God commands us to love Him and one another, and forgiveness is a big part of that command (Matthew 22:37-40). But if you look at what the Word says about forgiveness, you'll see that there is a reason why God wants you to deal with people this way.

Mark 11:25-26 makes it plain. Jesus says here, *"And when ye stand praying, forgive, if ye have aught against any: that your Father also which is in heaven may forgive you your trespasses. But if ye do not forgive, neither will your Father which is in heaven forgive your trespasses."* In Matthew 6:14-15 Jesus also says, *"For if ye forgive men their trespasses, your heavenly Father will also forgive you; But if ye forgive not men their trespasses, neither will your Father forgive your trespasses."* God isn't telling you to forgive people because He wants to make life hard for you. However, the Scriptures say that if you don't forgive people for the wrong things they've done to you, God won't forgive you.

You can't expect to have your prayers answered when you're holding on to aught and unforgiveness toward someone. You must get rid of that attitude before God can do some things on your behalf. I don't care how long you have been saved, or how good a person you think you are, you are going to need God's forgiveness often. But when you refuse to forgive others and choose to hold on to past grievances, you're setting yourself up for some bad things to happen. Every seed of unforgiveness you sow will eventually hurt you in the end.

Forgiveness: What It's Not

A common misconception about forgiveness is that it means that you make excuses for the wrong someone has done to you, or take the blame for someone's maltreatment of you. Sin is sin, no matter how it is packaged. There's no question about it or room to argue with what is wrong. Forgiveness doesn't try to make excuses for someone's bad behavior or justify it in some way. It simply recognizes that a person's action was wrong, and releases that person and situation to Jesus.

When you forgive someone, you don't try to take the blame for their conduct either. Forgiveness doesn't justify; it simply chooses to release. You simply say, "Lord, the way so-and-so treated me was wrong and it really hurt me. But even though what they did was hurtful, I *choose* to let it go. I *choose* to pardon them, Lord, because You told me to, and because You pardoned me of all my sins."

There are a lot of people who have gone through some horrendous things in their lives, from physical, mental and emotional abuse to having a family member taken away from them at the hands of another person. Situations like these will often cause people to become bitter, resentful and unforgiving and even justify their feelings. You hear them say, "You know, this happened to me, or that happened to me, and I just can't forgive them." The issue isn't that they *can't* forgive, but that they *won't* forgive. Unfortunately, these are the same people who are mad at the world, while the person who has wronged them has moved on with his or her life.

I'm not trying to downplay the emotions you experience when you are hurt. Your feelings may well be valid in light of what has happened to you; however, if your feelings are leading you to hold on to unforgiveness, you must release those feelings. Holding on to hurt is not worth jeopardizing what God wants to do in your life. Everyone has been hurt. The ability to move on is a decision you will have to make.

Again, please understand that forgiveness doesn't mean minimizing the wrong, or trying to sugarcoat it. Joseph never said that what his brothers did to him wasn't a big deal. The important part of the story is that he was able to extend forgiveness to them because he had the love of God in his heart. When it was time for Joseph to help the people who wronged him—his brothers—he was able to assist them without hesitation or resentment. He had a forgiving nature, which was in essence the love of God operating through him to bless those who had done him wrong.

So extending forgiveness will not always be easy; but it is a decision we all have to make on a daily basis. When you're hurt and upset about the way someone has treated you, you're in a pressure situation; but if you're going to experience victory under pressure you *have* to extend forgiveness. It won't always take away the hurt and it doesn't deny the past injury; however, it does keep the hurt from standing in the way of a fresh start.

A Heart Decision

One of the biggest mistakes that people make is thinking that forgiveness has anything to do with how you feel. As Christians, we don't live by our feelings. As with anything in the kingdom of

God, forgiveness is an act of your will and your faith in God's Word. It isn't an act of your flesh, so don't expect to feel some kind of warm fuzziness when you choose to forgive someone—you may be waiting a long time. When you first make the decision to forgive completely and walk in love, it won't be comfortable. But, when you realize that forgiveness isn't a feeling, you can better handle negative emotions when they arise.

This decision of the heart called forgiveness reflects your willingness to obey the Lord's commandment to walk in love. To refuse to do it is to disobey Him. Jesus goes so far as to say that we are to forgive those who wrong us *seven times seventy* times—that equals 490 times (Matthew 18:21-22). When you decide to forgive, you're choosing to act in line with God's love, and you can't help but reap an abundant harvest when you do that.

Over and over again in the Word, God admonishes us to walk in love. He is *Love*, and as His representatives, the level of love we demonstrate reflects our love for Him. Whether you are dealing with other Christians, or someone who doesn't know Jesus as his Lord and personal Savior, you have a responsibility to demonstrate the love of God. And, you have to understand that whenever you withhold forgiveness from someone you actually negate the power of forgiveness in your own life and it prevents you from walking in total freedom.

Ephesians 4:32 reminds us to be useful, helpful and kind to each other, and to forgive each other *readily* and *freely*. That means we are to be quick to forgive. Developing a lifestyle of forgiveness will take some training and practice, just like the world-class athlete who wins the gold medal. Believe me, you will have plenty of opportunities to build your forgiveness muscles and develop in the love of God.

You may be wondering how is it humanly possible to forgive

someone who has hurt you so bad that you can't even think about them without getting angry. Well, it isn't *humanly* possible. It requires tapping into the supernatural love of God within you. The good news is the same love that Jesus has is in your heart (Romans 5:5). Therefore, you *can* forgive even the worst offense that has been committed against you. It simply takes a decision.

We've all been here before; but again, I encourage you to go back to the life of Joseph. Genesis 47:11-12 says that Joseph supplied his family with food according to their needs. He also gave them a possession in the land of Egypt. Remember that these were the same brothers who attempted to kill him years before. But Joseph tapped into the love of God and it allowed him to give to the people who had wronged him. Not only did he give to them, he gave them the best part of the land.

Wouldn't you like to walk in this kind of love and power? To be able to be a blessing to those who have done you wrong is an awesome privilege and it will draw them to the Father like never before. When you look for opportunities to do this, you demonstrate the love of God in a powerful way, and you position yourself for increase and prosperity.

Get in Position

Increase, promotion and abundance are directly connected to the degree to which you walk in the love of God; you have to position yourself for these things to become a reality in your life. Making a quality decision to develop the love of God is the number one way to ensure victory every time. Forgiveness flows out of God's love, and as you cultivate this love in your life by acting in love when people hurt you, you cultivate forgiveness. The more you do it, the more people will see the character of God inside of you. To have this forgiving nature, you simply cannot allow bitterness, resentment, anger or vengeance into your heart.

It is also important that you forgive yourself for any mistakes you have made along the way, and not allow condemnation to set in. Oftentimes, the last person you forgive is yourself, but this is just as bad as not forgiving others. Refusing to forgive yourself only causes you to walk around with additional burdens. God doesn't want you to live that way, so it's very important that you activate forgiveness in your personal life.

Once you forgive yourself for any wrongs you may have committed toward others, go to God and ask Him to forgive you and He will. The Word of God says that He's faithful and just to forgive and cleanse you when you confess your sins to Him (1 John 1:9). Many times, people feel so bad about their past mistakes that they remain stuck in one place while God is trying to elevate them out of their situations. Don't fall into this trap. Forgive yourself, repent to God and move on.

> "INCREASE, PROMOTION AND ABUNDANCE ARE DIRECTLY CONNECTED TO THE DEGREE TO WHICH YOU WALK IN THE LOVE OF GOD."

There are rewards for the person who decides to forgive. One of them is that you will see God's vision for your life come to pass. Forgiveness clears the way for Him to get involved in your situation and remove the obstacles that may be standing in your way as you move toward your destiny. Any time you allow an outpouring of God's love to invade your life, Satan must get out of your way.

Joseph went from the pit to the palace because of his decision to honor God by walking in love. He saw the vision for his own life come to pass in due season because he refused to let a root of bitterness and unforgiveness creep into his thinking, despite the many opportunities he had to throw love out the window and seek revenge. He could have turned his brothers away, even though his family was experiencing famine in their land, but instead he chose the high road. He had plenty of obstacles in his way—jealousy, hatred, slavery, prison, false accusations and probably many more that aren't recorded in the Bible. But by forgiving his enemies, he was positioned for increase.

Joseph experienced the rewards of being a forgiving man—promotion, increase, prosperity and the opportunity to bless his family with the provision they needed. God will do the same for you if you let Him. Remember, His ultimate goal is to prosper you to the point that you can be a blessing to others. Matthew 6:33 says that when you seek God and His way of doing things, everything else you need to succeed will be added to you. Well, love is God's method of operation and to love others as God does guarantees supernatural progress in your life.

Forgiveness is not easy. There will be times when everything in you is screaming, "No! I just can't do this!" But that is the time when you must arrest your emotions and forgive anyway. It is a process. Your feelings won't always agree with your decision. In fact, sometimes you won't really feel like you have forgiven those who have wronged you. Sometimes, you'll have to confess the Word over your enemies several times a day. You may have to remind yourself that you have already forgiven them when anger, hurt feelings and hatred try to rear their ugly heads. But as you continue to practice the love of God, and continue to forgive by faith, you'll find yourself releasing love toward your enemies with ease.

I believe that the greatest reward of walking in forgiveness is that it opens the door for you to receive new peace, new love and certainly new freedom in God. Nothing compares to being able to say you have truly let go of an offense. Nothing is more satisfying than being able to bless someone who has hurt you and walk away knowing that your heart and mind are clear of all negativity you once harbored toward him or her. Only the love of God in you will enable you to do this. Keep in mind that living a lifestyle of forgiveness will cause you to reap a great harvest. Examine your life and, like Joseph, make the decision today to forgive. You may not see the results in your enemies right away, but you will experience victory while under the pressure to quit!

Favored to Win

6

6

Favored to Win

"For thou, Lord, wilt bless the righteous; with favour wilt thou compass him as with a shield" (Psalm 5:12).

Some people are successful in life because they are qualified, and others succeed because they are favored, plain and simple. Do you suppose that Tiger Woods, the golf champion, is favored to win and that is why he has been so successful? How about Michael Jordan, the famous basketball player? At the 1936 Summer Olympics in Berlin, was James Cleveland Owens, better known as "Jesse Owens," favored to win those four gold medals he received? What about Edwin Moses out of Morehouse College, who, by the mid 1980s, had an unbeaten winning streak of 102 races? Not many people know of Edwin Moses' life and victories on the track field; but it makes you wonder, was his winning streak just mere luck or was he favored to win? Only God truly knows.

I do know that when the Lord chooses to give you preferential treatment, there's no one and nothing that can stop it. Even though the world may value how qualified you are, God's system of operation doesn't work the same way. His favor surpasses any ability you may have in the natural realm. Take, for example, two people who are both equally qualified for a job, yet one man gets the position he desires over the other. There may be some other factors involved in a situation like that, but I believe that the key to a Christian's success over others is *favor*. God's favor on a man's life is the difference between success and failure.

Every Believer has the right to walk in the favor of God. If Jesus is your Lord and Savior, you have an edge, or advantage over those in the world. If you haven't made Jesus the Lord of your life, you, too, can tap into this key to victory by accepting Him into your heart. The moment you receive Jesus, God looks at you through "Jesus lenses," so to speak. As a Christian, your edge over the world lies in the fact that He dwells in you and imparts into your spirit the ability to love like He loves, do what He did and live like He lived on the earth. As a part of His family, His favor will follow you wherever you go, giving you success in every arena of life.

Joseph was a man who truly experienced the benefits of continually walking in God's supernatural favor. Only the favor of God could enable him to rise above such adverse circumstances the way that he did and go from being left for dead and sold into slavery, to being the second in command over the entire land of Egypt. His story is an inspiration to anyone who is going through challenges in life.

God moved Joseph from the pit to the palace, not because of how smart, handsome or charming he was, but because Joseph lived a life that was honorable before God. As a result, the Lord was with him at every turn, opening doors that no man could shut and clearing the hindrances out of Joseph's path. Because of Joseph's commitment to his God, he was blessed with an empowerment to prosper in everything he did. And no matter where he started out, he always reached a position of authority. You, too, can live this kind of life!

What is Favor?

Have you ever known someone who, no matter what situation they found themselves in, whether good or bad, they always seemed to come out on top? Sometimes it may seem that a person doesn't deserve favor, but yet they continue to experience it all the time. That's nothing to be upset about when you understand how much God loves each and every one of us.

Essentially, favor is preferential treatment; and as a child of God, you have a right to it. A person who knows they have favor says, "I'm the preferred one. I'm preferred over everyone else." Those sound like pretty bold and cocky statements, but they are the truth. You have to believe that you are favored before you can ever experience favor to the fullest. When you confess your preferred status over and over again, the reality of it will begin to sink into your heart and mind; you'll find yourself living a life of favor and experiencing the "perks" that come from maintaining a close relationship with your heavenly Father.

It is going to take more than your education, looks, personality and money to win big in life. The world system relies only on these qualities in order to get ahead. Christians have something better working for them that the world will never have—the favor of God. When His favor is working for you, it doesn't matter how many doors are slammed in your face, how many people tell you, "No" or how bad the situation looks. Favor will *always* propel you toward victory.

The Word of God has a lot to say about this preferential treatment from God. Psalm 102:13 says, *"Thou shalt arise, and have mercy upon Zion: for the time to favour her, yea, the set time, is come."* What this scripture is saying is that there is a set (or appointed) time for the favor of God to come on you; and that time is *now* if you'll receive it by faith!

You don't have to wait for something special to happen before you can start walking in favor; it is a reality now. Don't wait for something magical to happen in order to experience God working on your behalf. Instead, be proactive about walking in the favor of God. Grab hold of this truth and apply it to every situation you are facing right now that seems impossible. You may have creditors calling your house, or you may be facing a court case or custody battle. Perhaps you desire a better job or a promotion. Whatever the case may be, if you'll believe that God favors you, nothing will be able to stop you from coming out as a winner.

Look at Psalm 5:12: *"For thou, Lord, wilt bless the righteous; with favour wilt thou compass him as with a shield."* Here, the Word makes it clear that there is a direct connection between God's blessing, or empowerment to prosper, and His favor being on your life. First, the Scripture says that God blesses those who are in right standing with Him. As the righteousness of God, you are empowered to prosper and succeed; you have God's ability operating in your life. But the Bible goes on to say that the Father will cause His favor to *compass*, or surround you like a shield. That's good news because it means that you have favor with everyone with whom you come in contact. With your favor shield in place, nothing can stop you.

Favor With God vs. Favor With Man

Now Joseph was a man who truly walked in the favor of God. He also had favor with man. While you shouldn't make having favor with man your focus, the relationship you have with God will enable you to experience His favor with other people. The key is to seek Him *first*.

Please understand that people will let you down. That's why God doesn't want you trusting in man more than you trust Him. Don't go out of your way to please man, expecting some kind of reward. Make pleasing God your aim and everything else will follow. Your vertical relationship with the Father will

> "IT'S GOING TO TAKE MORE THAN YOUR EDUCATION, LOOKS, PERSONALITY AND MONEY TO WIN BIG IN LIFE."

determine the success you have in your relationships with people. Making *Him* the source of your success positions you for victory; He'll continue to open doors for you, even when other people won't.

Genesis 41:39 says that Pharaoh recognized Joseph as the most intelligent, understanding and wise man around. For the king of Egypt—a man who had no relationship with God—to say these things about Joseph, who was a covenant child of God, demonstrated that Joseph had favor working for him.

God's favor on your life will cause non-Christians to seek you out. They'll recognize that there is something different about you, and that you have something that they need and want. The presence of God on you will cause the most unlikely people to do things for you that both you and they never expected they would do.

Remember, it was Joseph's desire to please God that caused others to look upon him with favor. In fact, Joseph was favored by God at an early age and his brothers hated him for it. If you have siblings, you may be able to relate to this situation. Sometimes, in a large family, favoritism occurs between brothers and sisters. It isn't right and it isn't fair, but it happens nevertheless. This is what it was like in Joseph's family; he was his father's favorite child.

To make matters worse in his brothers' eyes, Joseph was a "dreamer" who had divinely granted visions from God, and he didn't hesitate to share those visions with his brothers. Of course, this made them angry, so much that they went so far as to plot his murder. Genesis 37:3-20 says:

> *Now Israel loved Joseph more than all his children, because he was the son of his old age: and he made him a coat of many colors. And when his brethren saw that their father loved him more than all his brethren, they hated him, and could not speak peaceably unto him. And Joseph dreamed a dream, and he told it his brethren: and they hated him yet the more...And they said one to another, Behold, this dreamer cometh. Come now therefore, and let us slay him, and cast him into some pit, and we will say, Some evil beast hath devoured him: and we shall see what will become of his dreams.*

Don't get me wrong; when the favor of God is on you, people will be jealous. Whether it is an ability, talent, special quality or just because other people esteem you highly, you have something that they want. You will be persecuted because of the preferential treatment you receive. But even in the midst of people coming against you, have confidence that whatever motivates them to try and hurt you won't stop you from being delivered out of trouble. Keep this in mind as you pursue the favor of God: **human behavior is never the key indicator as to whether or not God favors you.** Some people may not like you, but that doesn't mean that you don't have the favor of God on your life.

The Word says that when you find wisdom, you find life and

obtain favor (Proverbs 8:35). It also says that a *good man* obtains favor from God (Proverbs 12:2). Joseph was a good man and he was called wise and understanding by the king of Egypt. That meant that he had tapped into the wisdom of God and his character was pleasing in God's eyes. As a result, Joseph was honored by the Lord, and it was evident by the continual success that he enjoyed.

Please understand that this type of victory isn't limited to Joseph. In fact, as a Believer, you are in an even more advantageous position. God has cut a new and better covenant through Jesus Christ, and if you are in Him, He sees you just as He does Jesus—triumphant and victorious over the enemy and the pressures of life. Jesus is favored, and so are you!

Blessed to Be a Blessing

We've established the truth that it is the favor of God that will successfully move you through the challenging and uncomfortable situations in life and propel you from the back of the line to the front. Joseph was proof of this. But I want to show you something else about favor; it isn't available just so that *you* can get ahead. God favors you so that you can be a blessing to other people as well. When He puts you in a certain position, He expects that you will be a channel of His love and provision to those around you.

It is so awesome to know that once God moved Joseph into a position of power, he used it to benefit people. Not only that, he maximized the position he was in to provide for his family, specifically his brothers. The people who tried to kill him years before found themselves on the receiving end of God's provision and blessing. Yes, God even loves your enemies and wants to show His goodness to them through *you*. That's how wonderful He is!

Genesis 45:3-8 recounts the reunion of Joseph and his brothers:

> *And Joseph said to his brothers, I am Joseph! Is my father still alive? And his brothers could not reply, for they were distressingly disturbed and dismayed at [the startling realization that they were in] his presence...And he said, I am Joseph your brother, whom you sold into Egypt! But now, do not be distressed and disheartened or vexed and angry with yourselves because you sold me here, for God sent me ahead of you to preserve life...God sent me before you to preserve for you a posterity and to continue a remnant on the earth, to save your lives by a great escape and save for you many survivors.*

What Joseph's brothers planned for evil actually turned out for Joseph's good and theirs, too. God knew ahead of time that there would be a famine in their land. Even though the circumstances under which Joseph ended up in Egypt were less than favorable, God still used Joseph's experience to bring to pass His will and purpose in the earth at that time. He sent Joseph ahead of them to prepare a way of provision for them down the line. Had Joseph given up, caved in and quit, countless lives would have been lost. But because of his dedication to God and his determination to stick with the promises of God, he was favored. This opened the door for a generation of people to be saved from destruction.

I wonder whom God has favored you to bring out of captivity? There is someone out there who He wants you to bless because of the favored position in which He has put you. It may be someone on your job, a family member, your neighborhood or even a nation. No matter how many people the Lord has called you to impact, you can be certain that the favor you have now isn't just for you, but for someone else as well. God marked you as His favored child because He wants you to be a blessing to others.

It Pays to Do Things God's Way

The world may try and convince you that you are missing out on something when you live a life that pleases God, but that is a deception of Satan. The only thing you miss out on when you do things the Lord's way is the curse, which includes sickness, poverty, bondage, fear and every other form of destruction. I don't know anyone who would purposely want to be cursed, but when you turn away from God's Word, that is what will happen.

God doesn't want you to seek and obey Him because He's trying to keep you from having fun in life, but because He loves you and knows that if you stray from His path, the consequences will devastate you. It is impossible to ever experience the abundant, good life that He has planned for you when you don't respect the commandments He has set forth in His Word.

Favor just won't work for the man who refuses to put God and His Word first place in his life. Proverbs 3:1-4 says, *"My son, forget not my law; but let thine heart keep my commandments: For length of days, and long life, and peace, shall they add to thee. Let not mercy and truth forsake thee: bind them about thy neck; write them upon the table of thine heart: So shalt thou find favour and good understanding in the sight of God and man."*

In verses one and two of these scriptures, we see two commands and three blessings. The two commands are: (1) *forget not My law* and (2) *keep My commandments*. If we do these two things, the Word promises us three blessings: (1) length of days, (2) long life and (3) peace, or the wholeness of God.

In verses three and four, we are given three commands which will result in two blessings: *don't let mercy and truth forsake you, bind them about your neck, write them on your heart and you will receive favor and understanding.* Joseph demonstrated that God's system of operation works. His life was proof of the benefits of following God's commands.

When the Bible talks about not forgetting God's law and keeping His commandments, it means that He wants you to keep them at the forefront of your thinking at all times. It means letting those commandments sink deep into your heart and mind so that whenever a situation arises that challenges what God has told you, you don't bow to the pressure. That's what got Joseph through his fiery trials.

> "FAVOR IS A BYPRODUCT OF DOING THINGS GOD'S WAY."

By keeping God's commandments at the front of your mind and in your heart, and making them your priority, you are honoring Him. Obeying what He has said shows that His Word weighs heavier in your life than any temptation, trying circumstance or situation. The ability to do this only comes through continual meditation in God's Word as well as acting on it whenever you have a chance. The more you practice these things, the more ingrained in your spirit they will become until your automatic response to the pressures of life is to do what the Word says to do. This is when you will see the favor of God show up time and time again.

Yes, it is true that as a child of God, you are favored, and have a right to preferential treatment, but you have to do your part in order for that favor on your life to be activated. Favor is a byproduct of doing things God's way; there's no way around it. What price are you willing to pay to see this type of power working for you?

A lot of people want to experience the benefits of a relationship with God, but they aren't willing to pay the price.

Living wholeheartedly for God like Joseph did, means turning your back to those things that aren't pleasing in His sight, forsaking your old way of doing things, and following Him with everything you have. When you are presented with enticing situations, it means fleeing the scene, just like Joseph did from Potiphar's wife when she tried to seduce him. It even means being willing to go through persecution even though you know you are in the will of God for your life. When you are willing to maintain your integrity in the face of compromising situations, you demonstrate your faithfulness to the Father and His favor will *always* show up to deliver you.

God is not a respecter of persons. If He showed up in Joseph's life, He will do the same for you. But, will you honor Him with your life, time and obedience? If you do, He will cause you to triumph in every situation and circumstance when you recognize Him as your Source and obey what He has spoken in His Word.

Satan is a defeated foe, and therefore you have the ability to be victorious on a daily basis. You may have been let down by your parents, siblings, husband, wife or employer. Maybe you didn't have the greatest life growing up; however, I want you to know that you have Someone and *something* on your side that will put you over the top—God and His favor. Be encouraged today and know that just like Joseph, when you purpose to make God and your relationship with Him your first priority, His favor will show up and *always* cause you to experience victory under pressure!

Conclusion

Congratulations! Why? Because you accomplished something. What? Reaching the end of this book. I am making a big deal out of this accomplishment because you are closer to obtaining the victory you desire and deserve. Hopefully what you have read in this book has inspired you to pursue your dreams and destiny with greater fervor and intensity than before. Nothing can stop you when you make a sound decision to do what others are afraid to do to succeed. Others may be afraid to face their fears and struggles. You, on the other hand, have an advantage, and that is the knowledge of who you are and the love of God buried deep in your heart. Use that love to bless mankind in your pursuit of victory in every area of life, and in turn you'll be blessed.

Remember to maintain the sprit of victory at all cost. You can't afford to take on the mindset of a defeated person. You are *not* defeated; instead, you're a conqueror because that is who God made you to be.

When trouble and adversity come, don't run or ignore them. Face them with the intensity of a lion. In fact, develop *lion intensity*—the boldness to conquer regardless of the circumstance. Lion intensity requires becoming a victory-minded Christian. Think victorious thoughts and you will live a life of victory.

Not only should you think of victory all of the time, dream

big dreams as well so that you can win big in life. Don't even allow the "sky" to be the limit of your dreams. Regardless of the opposition you will no doubt face, have a clear vision of your life of success and victory. Do whatever it takes to remain motivated because *motivation* leads to *dedication*, which leads to *transformation*, which leads to *destination*!

God has so much in store for you, not just in heaven; I mean right here on earth. He wants to bless your socks off. That is why it is imperative that you not allow anything to distract your pursuit of a solid relationship with Him. Make Him your first priority because you are His. Remain faithful to God and trust Him to lead and direct you toward your destiny. Always live a disciplined life of prayer, Bible study and obedience, and you will reap the rewards of faithfulness to Him: prosperity, promotion and protection. Sounds good to me!

My life is evidence that God is real and that His goodness is great. The prosperity and blessing that I am experiencing are a direct result of my decision to live for the Lord wholeheartedly. I can't live prosperously and emotionally strong without my connection to Him. I know what it is to be disconnected from Him and I don't ever want to experience that again. That is why we as Christians must not only *hear* and *read* what the Word of God says; we must *apply it*. Application is the key to experiencing victory under pressure. The more we apply, the more we succeed. Now don't you want to succeed at everything you do in life? Of course you do! So what's stopping you?

Afterword: The Greatest Victory

The greatest victory you will ever experience in life is the victory over spiritual death. Spiritual death is simply separation from the life of God. It involves being disconnected from Him in spirit, soul and body. Those who have not made Jesus Christ the Lord over their lives are dead, spiritually speaking. It's like having a nice looking car with all of the nice trim work but without a working engine—it's not going anywhere.

You may be living a life of outward glamour, prosperity and prestige. From the outside, it seems as if you are living everyone's dream, but inwardly there is a void. Perhaps you're lonely even though you have lots of friends and loved ones around you. That is because there is only one Person Who can fill that void—God. Maybe you have tried to fill that void with other relationships that didn't work out, drugs, alcohol, your career, money...the list goes on. Unfortunately, you have experienced defeat as a result.

Cheer up! I have good news. God loves you despite your shortcomings. In fact, your failures aren't a big issue with Him, because He can help you work through them. If you are not born again, that is, if you have not accepted Jesus as Lord over your life, God's main concern is the condition of your spirit and soul. If you are not a born-again Believer, then you are separated from

Him spiritually. You cannot possibly hear clearly from Him and receive direction in life while you are in this spiritual condition. Your human spirit is not connected with His Spirit—His life and power. That is why victory seems so far out of reach at times.

The Word of God says, *"For whatsoever is born of God is victorious over the world; and this is the victory that conquers the world, even our faith. Who is it that is victorious over [that conquers] the world but he who believes that Jesus is the Son of God [who adheres to, trusts in, and relies on that fact]?"* (1 John 5:4-5, *The Amplified Bible*).

Based on this scripture, I invite you to change your life and change the direction in which you are heading. You have tried to live a victorious life, but as you can see, there is no true victory over the world without Jesus Christ. If you are not a born-again Believer but desire to be one, pray the following prayer with sincerity and conviction:

> *Dear Lord, in the name of Jesus, I accept You as my Heavenly Father. Your Word says that I can call on You and be saved from a life of sin and destruction. I call on You in faith, believing that You hear my prayer. According to Romans 10:9-10, I confess that Jesus is Lord and that You raised Him from the dead for my salvation. By faith I ask Jesus to come into my life, and to be my Lord and Savior. I believe that I am now a victorious Believer, and that I am no longer a sinner. Thank You for helping me to fulfill Your will for my life. In Jesus' name I pray. Amen!*

Welcome to a new life in Christ and in the love of God! Now, begin studying the Word of God to learn more about God's love and His plan for your life. Gradually begin developing a life of prayer, which is how you fellowship with your heavenly Father. Next, find a local church in your area that teaches the Word of

God without compromise. That is very important for your continued spiritual growth. Be mindful not to "feed" from a table that is not rich in the teaching of God's Word.

Lastly, begin spending time with fellow Christians who are dedicated to maintaining a firm relationship with God. They will be your support system as you mature in the things of God. If your old friends are living lives that are not pleasing to God, continue to love them, but do not allow them to draw you back into the life you have just made a decision to leave. One of the greatest changes in life that you can ever make is the people with whom you associate.

I would enjoy hearing from you and learning about your new life as a born-again Believer. Therefore, send me a letter to let me know of your decision by writing to:

Evett Davis
P.O. Box 6149
Augusta, Georgia 30916

Welcome to the Family of God!

About the Author

Evett Davis and her husband, Dr. Hardie Davis Jr., are Senior Pastors and Founders of Abundant Life Worship Center International, a non-denominational ministry located in Augusta, Georgia. Evett and her husband have one son, Benjamin. A graduate of the Medical College of Georgia with a Bachelor of Science degree in Medical Technology, Evett has a visibly enormous passion and love for people. She serves actively in her community in Augusta in various capacities.

Evett Davis is a woman of great wisdom, revelation and love for God. With an ability to teach the Word of God with simplicity and understanding, Evett strives diligently to inspire and impact the lives of people through the Word of God. She believes that many Christians live defeated lives simply because of a lack of understanding who they are in Christ. Evett's desire is to teach people who they are in Christ, inspire them to possess a spirit of victory, and to encourage them to walk in the favor of God.